Grade 4

Mathematics

Pupil Book 4B

PAT LILBURN
PAM RAWSON
PETER SULLIVAN

in consultation with
Elsie Kinavai
Alex Feeger

Department of Education Papua New Guinea

OXFORD
UNIVERSITY PRESS
AUSTRALIA & NEW ZEALAND

253 Normanby Road, South Melbourne, Victoria 3205, Australia

Oxford University Press is a department of the University of Oxford. It furthers the University's objective of excellence in research, scholarship, and education by publishing worldwide in

Oxford New York

Auckland Cape Town Dar es Salaam Hong Kong Karachi Kuala Lumpur Madrid Melbourne Mexico City Nairobi New Delhi Shanghai Taipei Toronto

With offices in

Argentina Austria Brazil Chile Czech Republic France Greece Guatemala Hungary Italy Japan Poland Portugal Singapore South Korea Switzerland Thailand Turkey Ukraine Vietnam

First published 1999
Reprinted 2003, 2008 (twice), 2010

ISBN 978 0 19 550863 5

Written by Pat Lilburn, Pam Rawson and Peter Sullivan
Writing consultants: Elsie Kinavai and Alex Feeger of the Curriculum Development Division of the Papua New Guinea Department of Education
Editorial and design consultant: John Hughes of the Papua New Guinea Department of Education

Cover and text design by Mary Kerr
Cover artwork by Gigs Wena
Illustrated by Petra Hanzak, Boris Silvestri and Wendy Gorton

Printed in China by Golden Cup Printing Co. Ltd
Published by Oxford University Press
Editorial Office: PO Box 7979, Boroko NCD,
Papua New Guinea

CONTENTS

SECRETARY'S MESSAGE

This pupil book is part of the new reformed mathematics program designed and written for use in Grade 4 classes in Community and Primary schools throughout Papua New Guinea.

The core materials consist of two pupil books called *Grade 4 Mathematics Pupil Book* 4A and *Grade 4 Mathematics Pupil Book* 4B. They are accompanied by the *Grade 4 Mathematics Teacher's Resource Book*. They replace the MACS series now in use.

In the Mathematics program children are first taught mathematics by using real objects. Later, the children will use pictures of objects. Finally, the children will use number symbols to represent these objects. Always allow your pupils to use real objects during their mathematics lessons if they want to. Teach the concepts in the context of real life situations as this leads to an appreciation of the everyday use of mathematics skills and knowledge. The children will decide when they do not need the help of real objects any longer. Remember, when children use real objects, they will understand mathematics better. This program also encourages the children to solve their own problems and make their own decisions with confidence. In order to learn these skills, the children should talk about what they are doing in every lesson. Since learning is most effective when it has meaning and is enjoyable, allow the children to use the language that they are most comfortable with.

However, in Grade 4 more English should be used together with the vernacular and other languages to aid understanding of new and difficult concepts.

Finally, the National Department of Education wants teachers to be flexible in programming and timetabling to cater for the different abilities of children and multigrade teaching situations. This book shows you some strategies to help satisfy these needs.

Peter M. Baki

PETER M. BAKI

Secretary of Education

Work out how many of the small shapes are needed to cover the other shape.

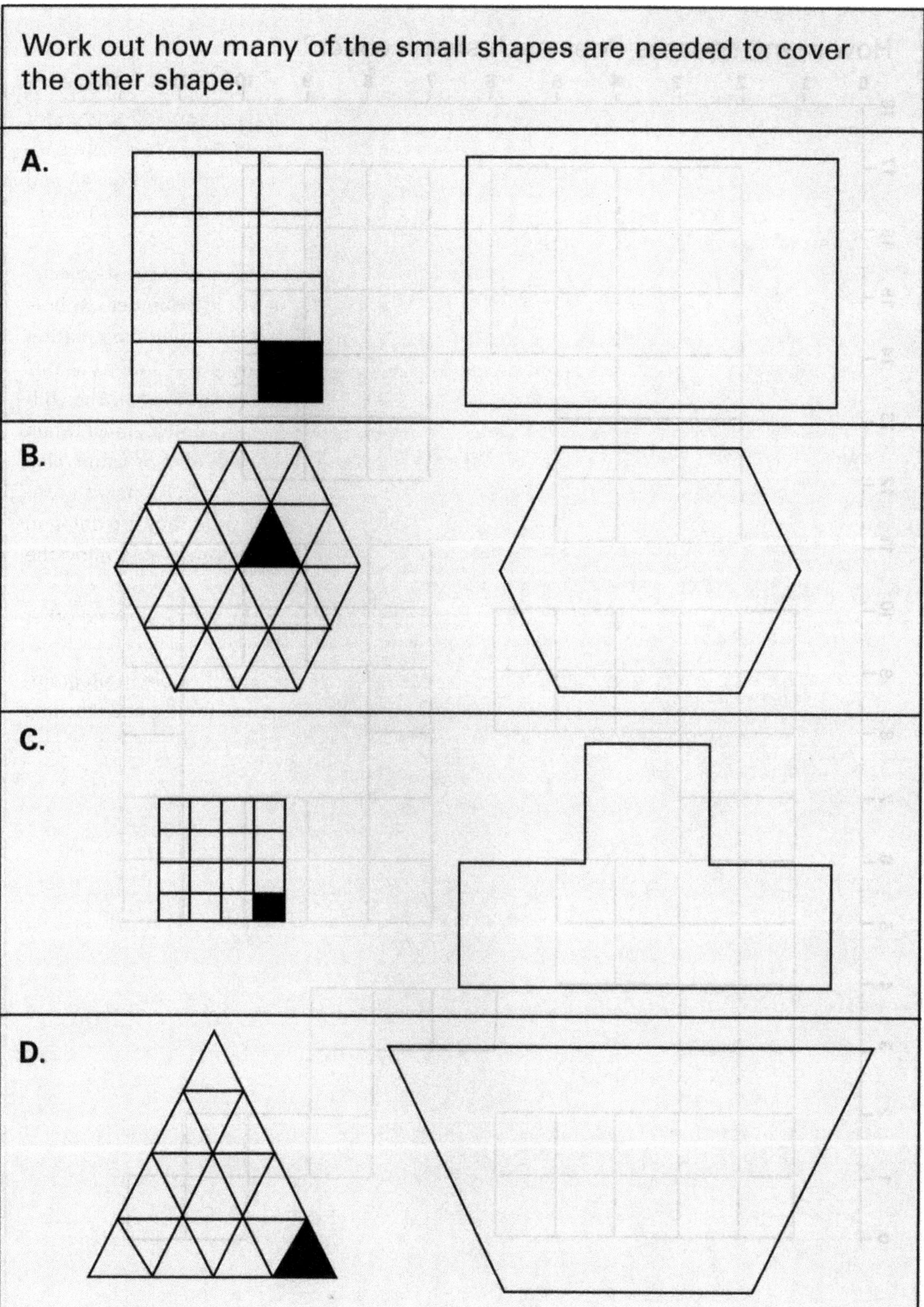

How many squares does each shape cover?

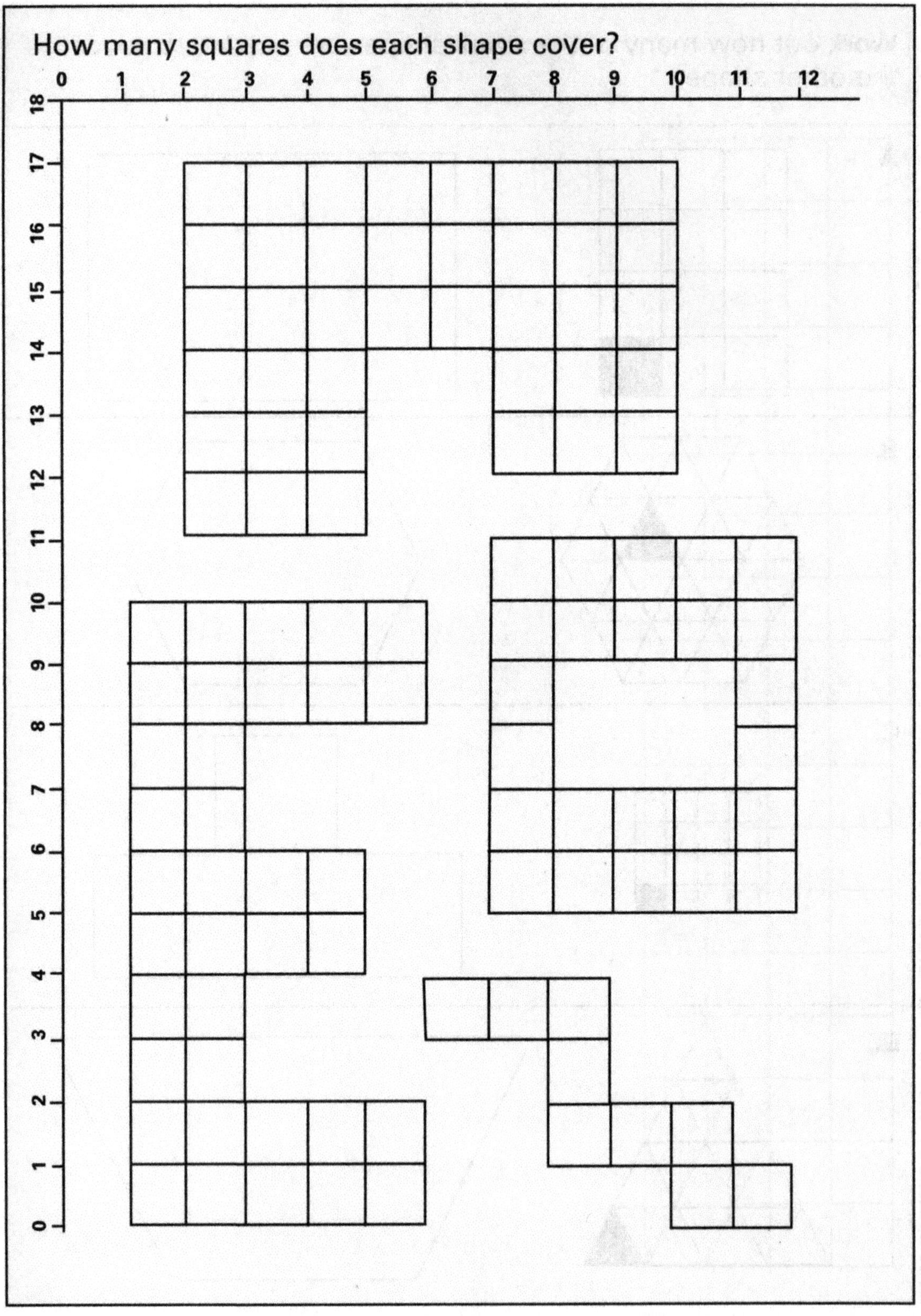

Use this centimetre grid to find the area of some objects.

Find the area of these rectangles.

a

b

c

d

e

f

g

Find the area of these shapes.

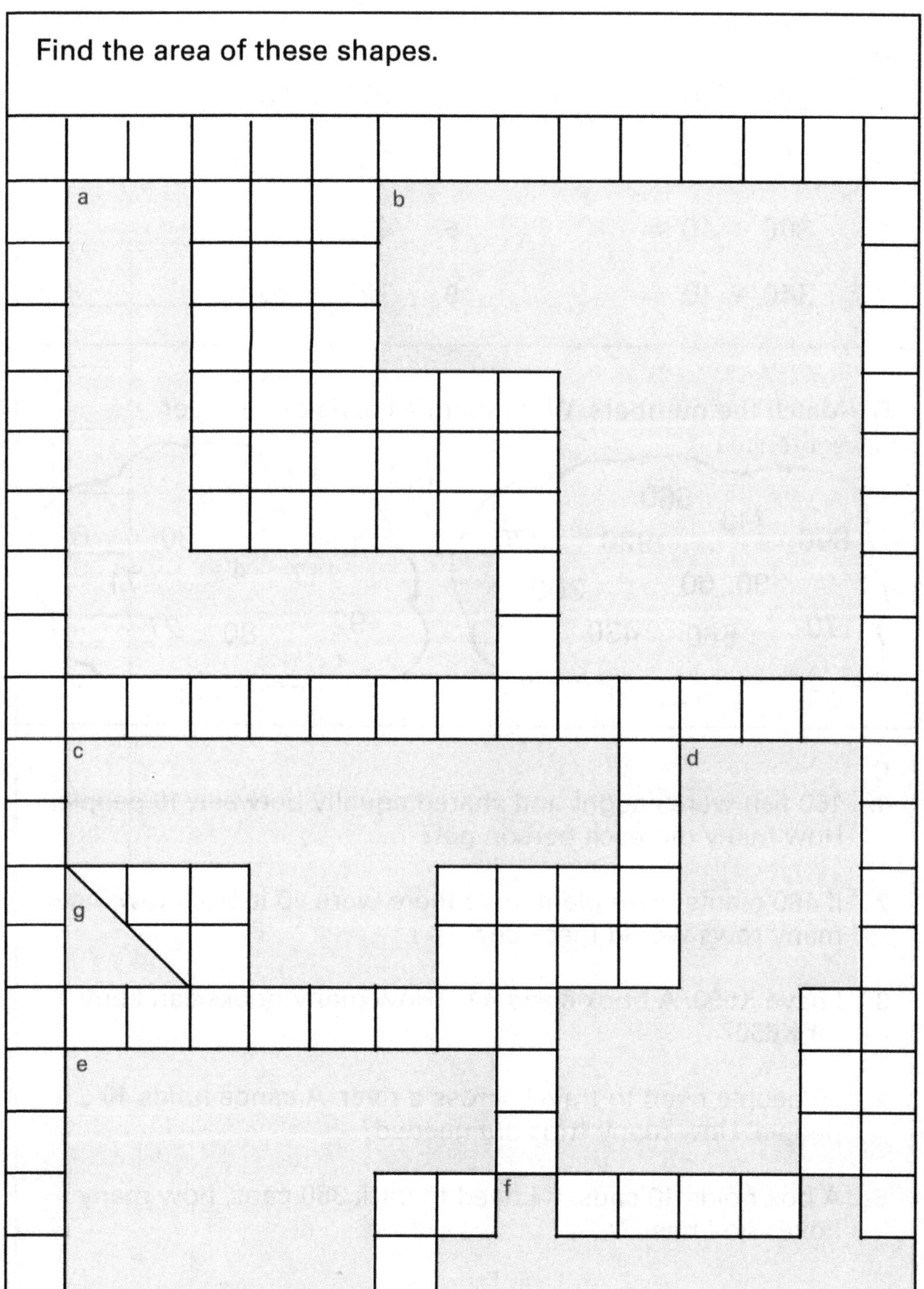

A

1. 680 ÷ 10 = **2.** 270 ÷ 10 =

3. 550 ÷ 10 = **4.** 390 ÷ 10 =

5. 800 ÷ 10 = **6.** 410 ÷ 10 =

7. 340 ÷ 10 = **8.** 120 ÷ 10 =

B Match the numbers. Write them as division number sentences.

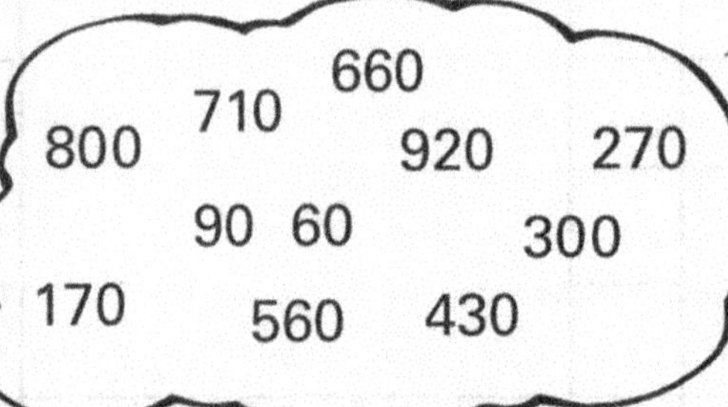

÷ 10

56 66 9 30 6 17 43 71 92 80 27

C

1. 160 fish were caught and shared equally between 10 people. How many did each person get?

2. If 480 plants were planted so there were 10 in each row, how many rows would there be?

3. I have K650. A book costs K10. How many books can I buy for K650?

4. 50 people need to travel across a river. A canoe holds 10 people. How many trips are needed?

5. A box holds 10 cans. If I need to pack 350 cans, how many boxes do I need?

1. We harvest 355 kaukau. How many piles of 3 can we make?
2. A big school has 85 children in grade 4. How many teams with 5 children each can be made? How many teams of 6 can be made?
3. 84 wheelbarrows of soil were taken away when 6 people were making a garden. They each removed the same amount of soil. How many wheelbarrow loads did each person take?
4. A gardener has 196 seeds to plant in 4 garden beds. He plants the same number in each bed. How many seeds are in each bed?
5. Two 10 year old children pick 139 tomatoes. How many bags with 6 tomatoes each can they pack?
6. 68 people were being taken in canoes across a river. Each canoe held 5 people. How many canoes were needed?
7. We have to buy 152 cans of drinks. They are packed in sixes. How many packs will we need?

A Use multiplication to check if these divisions are correct.

1. $4\overline{)7\overset{3}{6}}$
   19

2. $5\overline{)8\overset{3}{5}}$
   18

3. $3\overline{)5\overset{2}{8}}$
   19 rem. 3

4. $6\overline{)8\overset{2}{4}}$
   14

5. $3\overline{)17\overset{2}{7}}$
   59

6. $4\overline{)10\overset{2}{6}}$
   27

7. $5\overline{)21\overset{6}{6}}$
   39 rem. 1

8. $6\overline{)128}$
   21 rem. 2

9. $4\overline{)3\overset{1}{1}\overset{1}{9}}$
   158 rem. 3

B Fill in the missing numbers.

1. 36 ÷ ☐ = ☐

2. 100 ÷ ☐ = ☐

3. ☐ ÷ ☐ = 120

4. I have 48 guavas I wish to sell. I will group them in piles. How many can I put in each pile, and how many piles will I have?

In your exercise book, write these sums and work out the answers.

A

1. 15×8

2. 23×8

3. 31×8

4. 92×8

5. 35×8

6. 17×8

7. 64×8

8. 46×8

9. 78×8

10. 24×8

11. 77×8

12. 55×8

B

1. $8\overline{)48}$

2. $8\overline{)200}$

3. $8\overline{)176}$

4. $8\overline{)336}$

5. $8\overline{)424}$

6. $8\overline{)672}$

7. $8\overline{)664}$

8. $8\overline{)848}$

9. $8\overline{)824}$

10. $8\overline{)400}$

11. $8\overline{)104}$

12. $8\overline{)576}$

In your exercise book, write these sums and work out the answers.

A

1. $\begin{array}{r} 15 \\ \times 9 \\ \hline \end{array}$

2. $\begin{array}{r} 23 \\ \times 9 \\ \hline \end{array}$

3. $\begin{array}{r} 31 \\ \times 9 \\ \hline \end{array}$

4. $\begin{array}{r} 92 \\ \times 9 \\ \hline \end{array}$

5. $\begin{array}{r} 35 \\ \times 9 \\ \hline \end{array}$

6. $\begin{array}{r} 17 \\ \times 9 \\ \hline \end{array}$

7. $\begin{array}{r} 64 \\ \times 9 \\ \hline \end{array}$

8. $\begin{array}{r} 46 \\ \times 8 \\ \hline \end{array}$

9. $\begin{array}{r} 78 \\ \times 9 \\ \hline \end{array}$

10. $\begin{array}{r} 24 \\ \times 9 \\ \hline \end{array}$

11. $\begin{array}{r} 77 \\ \times 9 \\ \hline \end{array}$

12. $\begin{array}{r} 55 \\ \times 9 \\ \hline \end{array}$

B

1. $9\overline{)36}$

2. $9\overline{)360}$

3. $9\overline{)288}$

4. $9\overline{)198}$

5. $9\overline{)387}$

6. $9\overline{)297}$

7. $9\overline{)207}$

8. $9\overline{)495}$

9. $9\overline{)558}$

10. $9\overline{)648}$

11. $9\overline{)927}$

12. $9\overline{)936}$

1. In your exercise book, write which number is shown by the MAB pieces. Draw pictures to show the other two numbers.

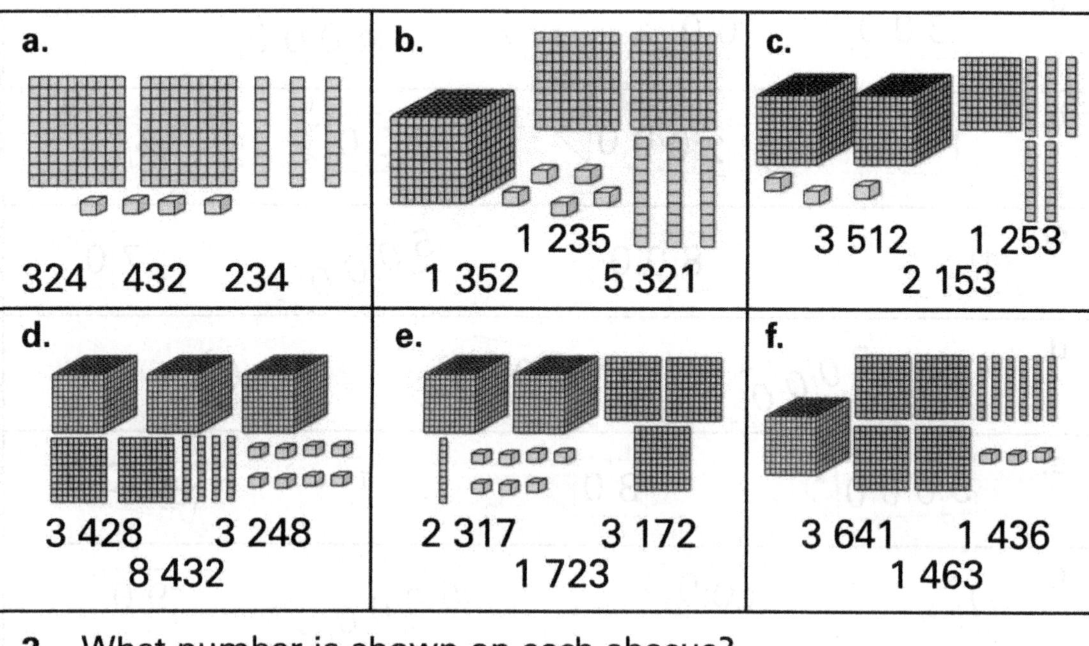

2. What number is shown on each abacus?

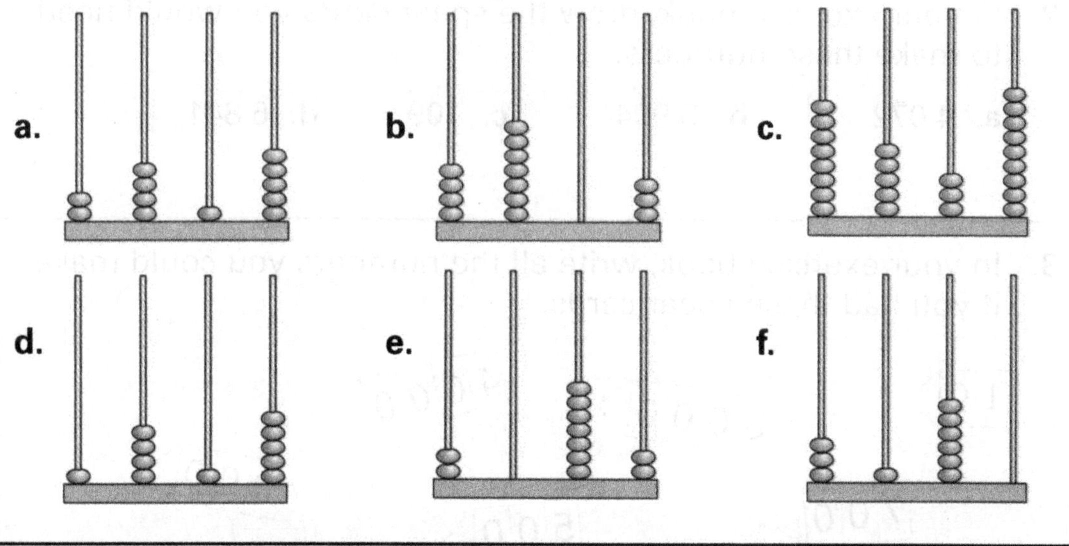

3. In your exercise book, draw MAB pieces to show each of the numbers in question 2.

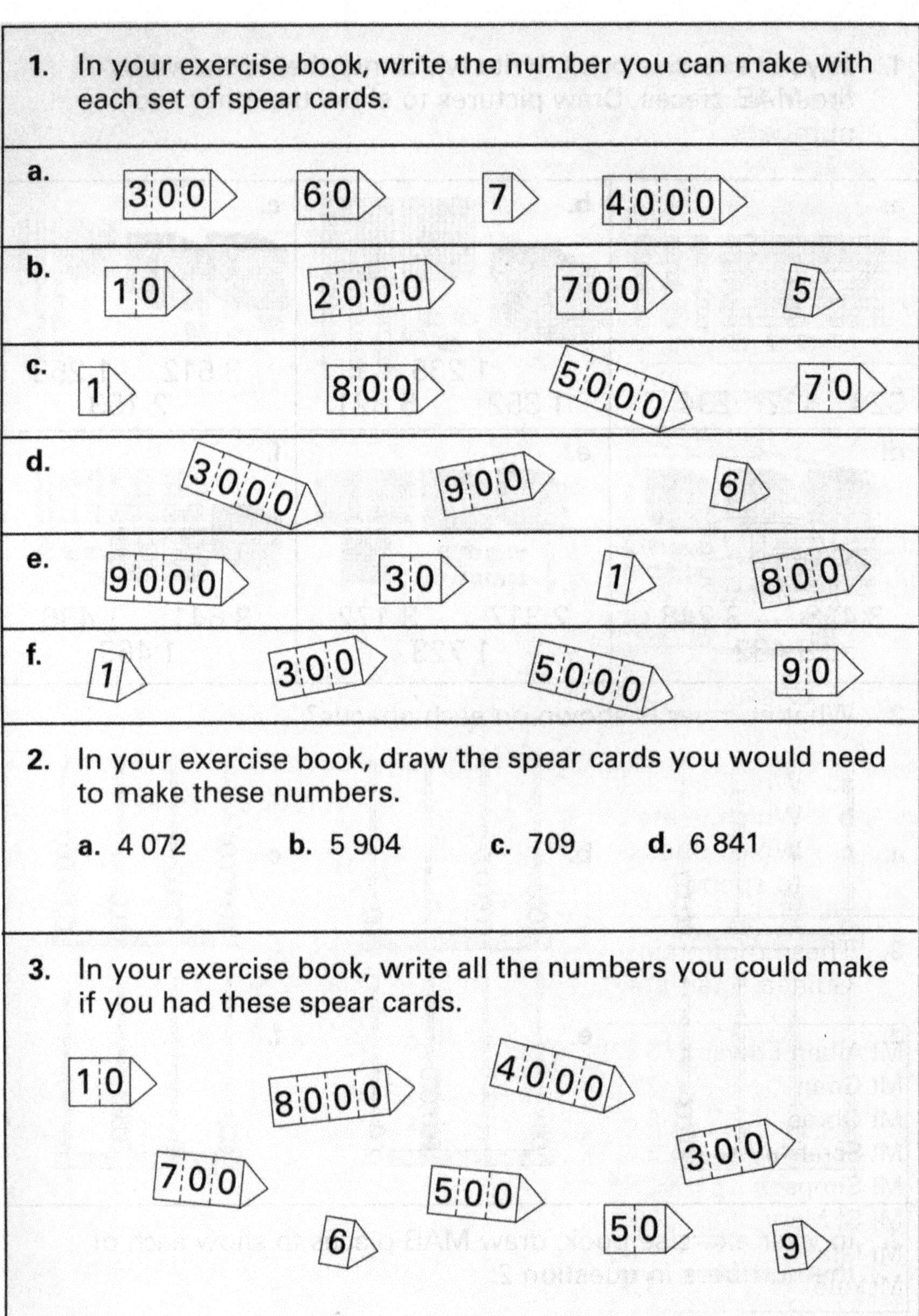

1. In your exercise book, write the number you can make with each set of spear cards.

a. 300 60 7 4000

b. 10 2000 700 5

c. 1 800 5000 70

d. 3000 900 6

e. 9000 30 1 800

f. 1 300 5000 90

2. In your exercise book, draw the spear cards you would need to make these numbers.

a. 4 072 **b.** 5 904 **c.** 709 **d.** 6 841

3. In your exercise book, write all the numbers you could make if you had these spear cards.

10 8000 4000 700 500 300 6 50 9

1. In your exercise book, write the dates on these coins in order, from past to present.

2.

a. Which car is most expensive?
b. Which is the cheapest?
c. Which ones could you choose from if you had K8 200 to spend?

3. These mountains are in the Central Province of Papua New Guinea. Their heights are shown in metres.

Mt Albert Edward	3 989
Mt Goan	2 801
Mt Obree	3 055
Mt Scratchly	3 480
Mt Simpson	2 880
Mt St Mary	3 656
Mt Tafa	2 697
Mt Yule	3 308

a. Which mountain is highest?
b. How many mountains are lower than 3 200 metres?
c. How many mountains are higher than Mt. Obree?
d. Write the mountain heights in order from lowest to highest.

1. In your exercise book, write the biggest and the smallest number you can make with each group of digits.

a	b	c
6 7 4 3	1 6 7 9	9 7 6 3
d	**e**	**f**
0 4 2 6	8 4 3 2	4 1 8 5
g	**h**	**i**
6 6 1 3	5 7 2 0	6 2 9 4

2. Read these numbers.

3 521, 1 560, 637, 567, 259, 5 769, 2 034, 4 028, 636, 238, 1 167, 6 772, 7 056, 2 153, 506, 613, 8 567

In your exercise book write:

a. the numbers that have a 3 in the tens place

b. the numbers that have 0 in the hundreds place.

c. the numbers that have 7 in the units place.

d. the numbers that have no thousands.

A Write these words as numbers in your exercise book.

Six thousand five hundred and twelve

Four thousand two hundred and sixty eight

Seven thousand and ninety six

Three thousand one hundred and fifty two

Nine thousand four hundred and seven

Five thousand six hundred and seventy one

B Copy these price tags into your exercise book and write each one in words.

K2 068

K8 415

K6 372

K5 150

K3 109

K2 589

C Copy this counting pattern into your exercise book and fill the gaps.

Four thousand and forty six, Four thousand and sixty six, ________, Four thousand, one hundred and six, Four thousand one hundred and twenty six, ________, Four thousand, one hundred and sixty six, Four thousand, one hundred and eighty six.

Look at these shapes. Find which ones are the same. Write your answers in your exercise book. Draw the shapes beside your answers.

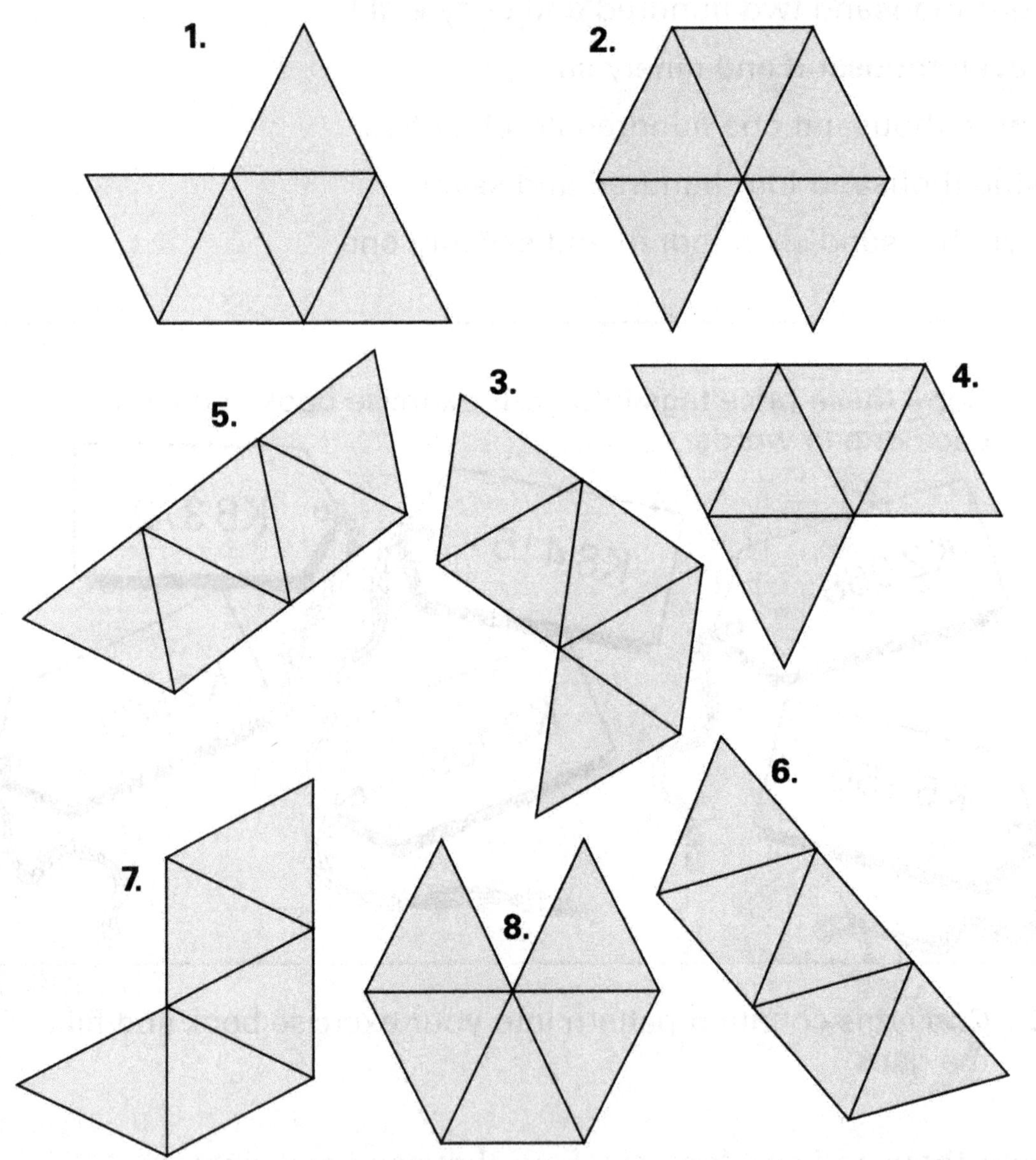

Use five paper triangles to make each of these shapes. Now use your triangles to make some new shapes. Copy your new shapes into your exercise book.

1. In your exercise book, write the name of the shape you can see in each picture. Draw the outline of each shape beside its name.

2. Draw something else that has the same shape as each of these pictures.

1. Make these shapes with sticks and joiners.

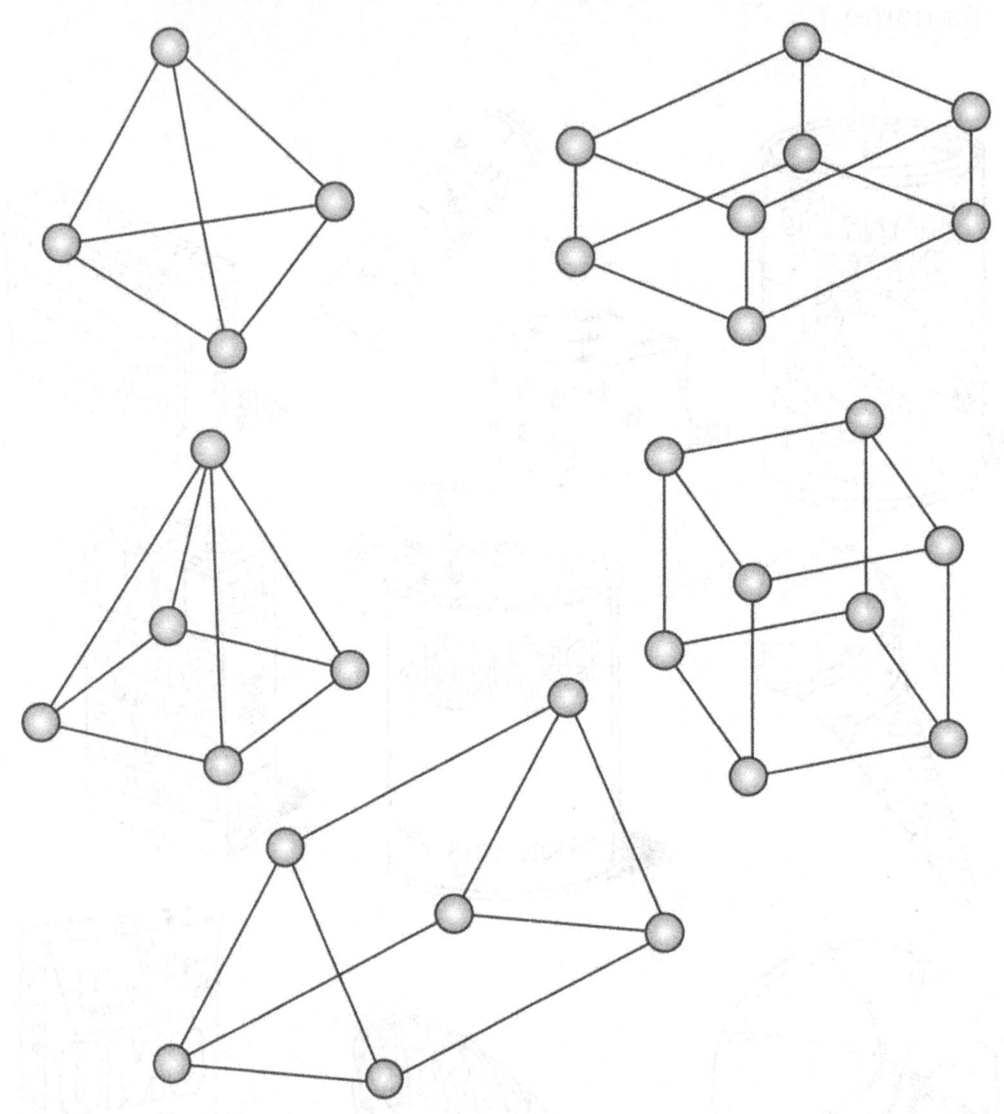

2. Draw your shapes in your exercise book.

3. Write how many faces and how many edges each shape has.

1. In your exercise book, write what shapes you can see in each of these buildings.

2. Choose one of the buildings. Draw three pictures of it: one from the front, one from above and one from the side.

1. In your exercise book, draw what shape you would see if you looked down on each of these buildings.

2. Choose one of the buildings. Draw three pictures of it: one from the front, one from above and one from the side.

This is the calendar for the year 2010. Study it carefully and then answer the questions in your exercise book.

JANUARY

M		4	11	18	25
T		5	12	19	26
W		6	13	20	27
T		7	14	21	28
F	1	8	15	22	29
S	2	9	16	23	30
S	3	10	17	24	31

FEBRUARY

M	1	8	15	22
T	2	9	16	23
W	3	10	17	24
T	4	11	18	25
F	5	12	19	26
S	6	13	20	27
S	7	14	21	28

MARCH

M	1	8	15	22	29
T	2	9	16	23	30
W	3	10	17	24	31
T	4	11	18	25	
F	5	12	19	26	
S	6	13	20	27	
S	7	14	21	28	

APRIL

M		5	12	19	26
T		6	13	20	27
W		7	14	21	28
T	1	8	15	22	29
F	2	9	16	23	30
S	3	10	17	24	31
S	4	11	18	25	

MAY

M	31	3	10	17	24
T		4	11	18	25
W		5	12	19	26
T		6	13	20	27
F		7	14	21	28
S	1	8	15	22	29
S	2	9	16	23	30

JUNE

M		7	14	21	28
T	1	8	16	22	29
W	2	9	17	23	30
T	3	10	18	24	
F	4	11	19	25	
S	5	12	20	26	
S	6	13	21	27	

JULY

M		5	12	19	26
T		6	13	20	27
W		7	14	21	28
T	1	8	15	22	29
F	2	9	16	23	30
S	3	10	17	24	31
S	4	11	18	25	

AUGUST

M	30	2	9	16	23
T	31	3	10	17	24
W		4	11	18	25
T		5	12	19	26
F		6	13	20	27
S		7	14	21	28
S	1	8	15	22	29

SEPTEMBER

M		6	13	20	27
T		7	14	21	28
W	1	8	15	22	29
T	2	9	16	23	30
F	3	10	17	24	
S	4	11	18	25	
S	5	12	19	26	

OCTOBER

M		4	11	18	25
T		5	12	19	26
W		6	13	20	27
T		7	14	21	28
F	1	8	15	22	29
S	2	9	16	23	30
S	3	10	17	24	31

NOVEMBER

M	1	8	15	22	29
T	2	9	16	23	30
W	3	10	17	24	
T	4	11	18	25	
F	5	12	19	26	
S	6	13	20	27	
S	7	14	21	28	

DECECEMBER

M		6	13	20	27
T		7	14	21	28
W	1	8	15	22	29
T	2	9	16	23	30
F	3	10	17	24	31
S	4	11	18	25	
S	5	12	19	26	

1. On what day of the week will Christmas be in 2010?
2. Is 2010 a leap year?
3. How many Fridays are there in May 2010?
4. Write about your birthday in 2010.
5. What is the date of the 1st Sunday in September 2010?
6. How many school days will there be in February 2010?
7. On what day of the week will New Years Eve be in 2010?
8. What might you be doing on 14th June 2010?

This is a time chart of the Wedau people. Study it carefully, then answer the questions in your exercise book.

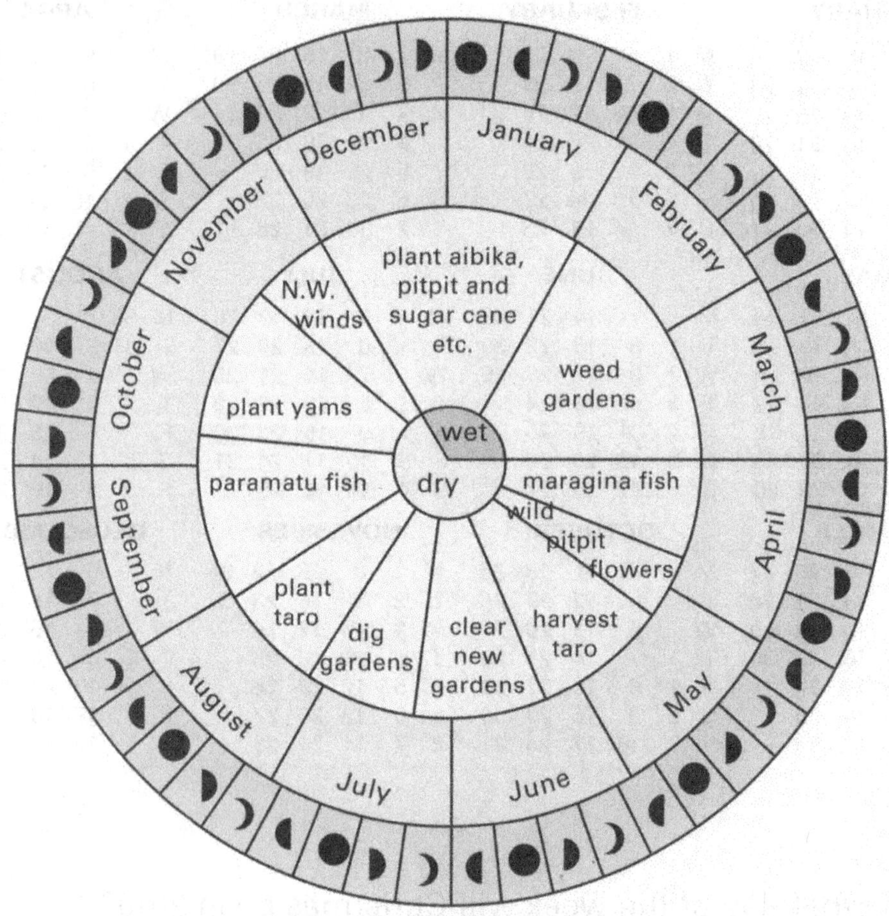

1. Which months are the dry season?
2. Is May a good month for planting?
3. When do the Wedau people fish for paramatu?
4. In which months do the Wedau people collect pit pit flowers?
5. How many times in the year is there a half moon?
6. What happens in your local area in June? Is this the same as for the Wedau people?

Study this calendar carefully, then answer the questions in your exercise book.

JANUARY					
M		4	11	18	25
T		5	12	19	26
W		6	13	20	27
T		7	14	21	28
F	1	8	15	22	29
S	2	9	16	23	30
S	3	10	17	24	31

FEBRUARY				
M	1	8	15	22
T	2	9	16	23
W	3	10	17	24
T	4	11	18	25
F	5	12	19	26
S	6	13	20	27
S	7	14	21	28

MARCH					
M	1	8	15	22	29
T	2	9	16	23	30
W	3	10	17	24	31
T	4	11	18	25	
F	5	12	19	26	
S	6	13	20	27	
S	7	14	21	28	

APRIL					
M		5	12	19	26
T		6	13	20	27
W		7	14	21	28
T	1	8	15	22	29
F	2	9	16	23	30
S	3	10	17	24	31
S	4	11	18	25	

MAY					
M	31	3	10	17	24
T		4	11	18	25
W		5	12	19	26
T		6	13	20	27
F		7	14	21	28
S	1	8	15	22	29
S	2	9	16	23	30

JUNE					
M		7	14	21	28
T	1	8	16	22	29
W	2	9	17	23	30
T	3	10	18	24	
F	4	11	19	25	
S	5	12	20	26	
S	6	13	21	27	

JULY					
M		5	12	19	26
T		6	13	20	27
W		7	14	21	28
T	1	8	15	22	29
F	2	9	16	23	30
S	3	10	17	24	31
S	4	11	18	25	

AUGUST					
M	30	2	9	16	23
T	31	3	10	17	24
W		4	11	18	25
T		5	12	19	26
F		6	13	20	27
S		7	14	21	28
S	1	8	15	22	29

SEPTEMBER					
M		6	13	20	27
T		7	14	21	28
W	1	8	15	22	29
T	2	9	16	23	30
F	3	10	17	24	
S	4	11	18	25	
S	5	12	19	26	

OCTOBER					
M		4	11	18	25
T		5	12	19	26
W		6	13	20	27
T		7	14	21	28
F	1	8	15	22	29
S	2	9	16	23	30
S	3	10	17	24	31

NOVEMBER					
M	1	8	15	22	29
T	2	9	16	23	30
W	3	10	17	24	
T	4	11	18	25	
F	5	12	19	26	
S	6	13	20	27	
S	7	14	21	28	

DECECEMBER					
M		6	13	20	27
T		7	14	21	28
W	1	8	15	22	29
T	2	9	16	23	30
F	3	10	17	24	31
S	4	11	18	25	
S	5	12	19	26	

1. How many days are there from 24th April until 16th May?
2. How many days are there from 12th September until 23rd December?
3. How many days are there until the end of the year?
4. How many days are in this year?
5. What will be the date 30 days before Good Friday?
6. How many days are there from 1st January until your birthday?
7. How many days are in the dry months?
8. If school finished 3 weeks before Christmas, what date would that be?

Make up some questions about this timetable and write them in your book, e.g.
When does the 7.00 a.m. plane arrive in Bialla?

Time table for one of the 3rd level airlines
From Monday to Saturday

Flight	Departure	From	To	Arrival
400	7.30 a.m	HGU	GKA	8.00 a.m.
B200	8.15 a.m	GKA	LAE	8.45 a.m.
401	7.00 a.m.	RAB	BAA	7.35 a.m.
EMB	7.45 a.m.	BAA	HKN	8.00 a.m.
	8.20 a.m.	HKN	LAE	9.40 a.m.
	10.10 a.m.	LAE	GKA	10.40 a.m.
	10.55 a.m.	GKA	HGU	11.25 a.m.
420	6.45 a.m.	RAB	ATN	7.00 a.m.
DHT	7.15 a.m.	ATN	LNV	7.35 a.m.
	7.45 a.m.	LNV	KVG	8.25 a.m.
	9.10 a.m.	KVG	LNV	9.50 a.m.
	10.00 a.m.	LNV	RAB	10.30 a.m.

BAA Bialla
GKA Goroka
HKN Hoskins
KVG Kavieng
LAE Lae
LNV Londolovit
HGU Mount Hagen
ATN Namatanai
POM Port Moresby
RAB Rabaul (Tokua)

Use the clocks to help you work out how long each story takes. Write the answers in your exercise book.

EMTV Programme Guide

6.00 a.m.	Nine Early News	6.00 p.m.	National EMTV News
7.00 a.m.	Today Show	6.30 p.m.	A Current Affairs
8.00 a.m.	Here's Humphrey	6.57 p.m.	Update of News
9.00 a.m.	Test Pattern	7. 00 p.m.	Dr Quinn
1.30 p.m.	Midday Show	8.00 p.m.	Tok Pisin Nius
3.00 p.m.	Kids Kona	8.05 p.m.	Neighbours
4.00 p.m.	Good Sports	8.35 p.m.	Babylon 5
4.57 p.m.	EMTV Toksave	9.35 p.m.	V-Mini series
5.00 p.m.	Home and Away	10.27 p.m.	EMTV Toksave
5.29 p.m.	EMTV News Break	10.35 p.m.	D. Letterman Show
5.30 p.m.	Sale of the Century	11.35 p.m.	National EMTV News
		12.05 a.m.	Test Pattern

Use the TV guide to work out some time questions of your own.

In your exercise book, write the answers to these questions.

1. What time will it be half an hour before each of the times shown?
2. What time will it be one and a half hours after each of the times shown?
3. Write the times shown on the clocks in order from earliest to latest.
4. Which clock shows the time closest to when you get up in the morning?

For each Frame, copy the odd one out into your exercise book and say why it is different.

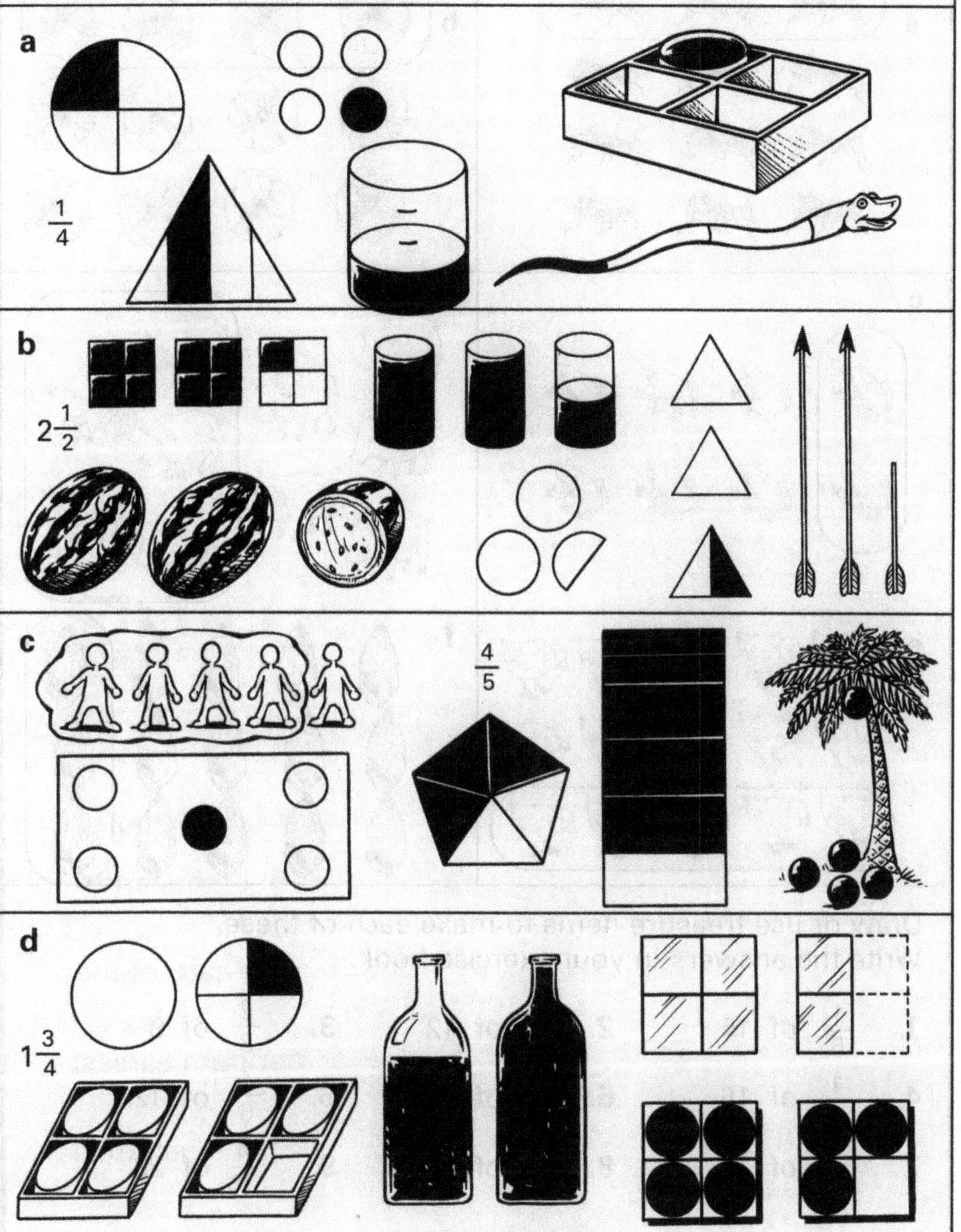

Find out what fraction of each group is circled and write it in your exercise book.

a

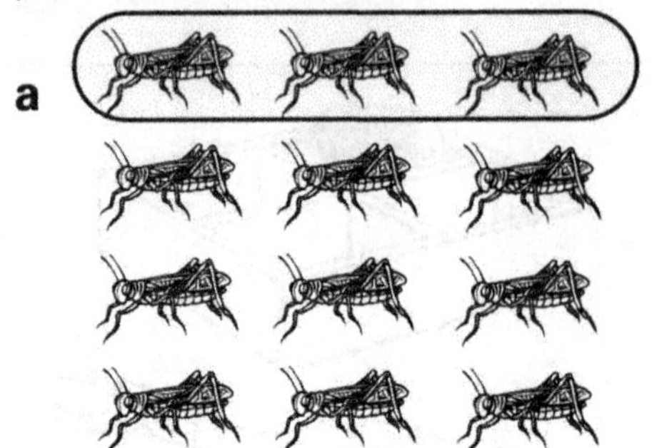

b

c

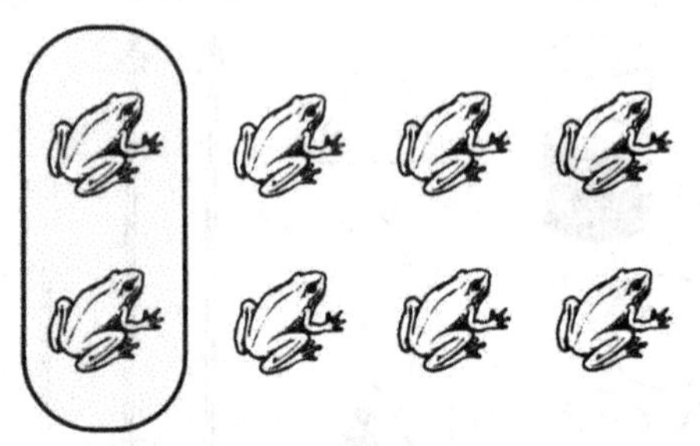

d

e

f

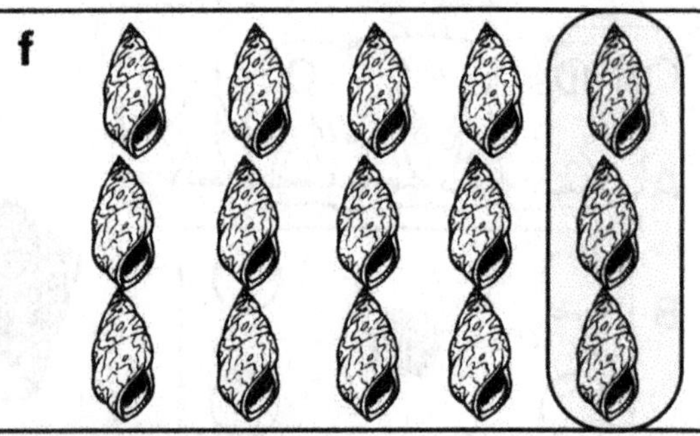

Draw or use treasure items to make each of these.
Write the answers in your exercise book.

1. $\frac{1}{5}$ of 15	**2.** $\frac{1}{3}$ of 12	**3.** $\frac{2}{3}$ of 9
4. $\frac{1}{4}$ of 16	**5.** $\frac{3}{4}$ of 8	**6.** $\frac{4}{6}$ of 12
7. $\frac{3}{5}$ of 10	**8.** $\frac{5}{6}$ of 18	**9.** $\frac{4}{10}$ of 20

In your exercise book, write the answers to these questions.
Use the pictures to help you.

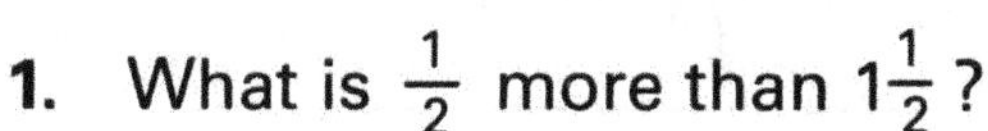

1. What is $\frac{1}{2}$ more than $1\frac{1}{2}$?

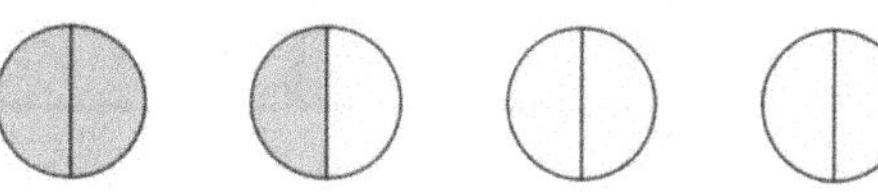

2. What is $\frac{1}{2}$ less than 3?

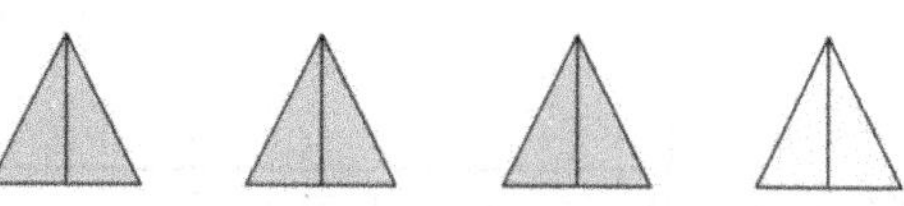

3. What is $\frac{1}{2}$ less than 4?

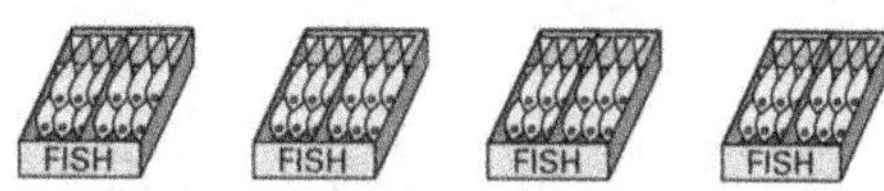

4. What is $\frac{1}{4}$ less than 2?

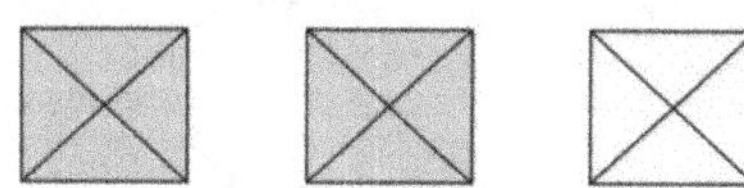

5. What is $\frac{1}{4}$ more than $1\frac{3}{4}$?

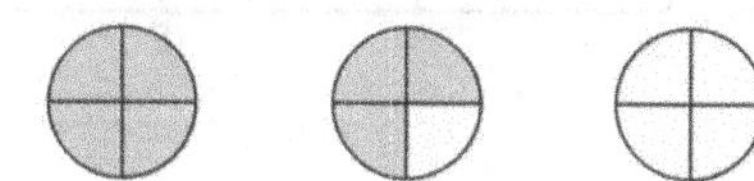

6. What is $\frac{1}{2}$ more than $4\frac{1}{2}$?

Complete these number patterns.

A	$\frac{1}{4}$	$\frac{2}{4}$	$\frac{3}{4}$	____	____	____	____
B	$\frac{1}{3}$	$\frac{2}{3}$	1	____	____	____	____
C	$\frac{1}{2}$	1	$1\frac{1}{2}$	____	____	____	____
D	6	$5\frac{1}{2}$	5	____	____	____	____
E	4	$4\frac{1}{3}$	$4\frac{2}{3}$	____	____	____	____
F	5	$4\frac{3}{4}$	$4\frac{1}{2}$	____	____	____	____

What fraction is shown on each number line? Write the answers in your exercise book.

a. 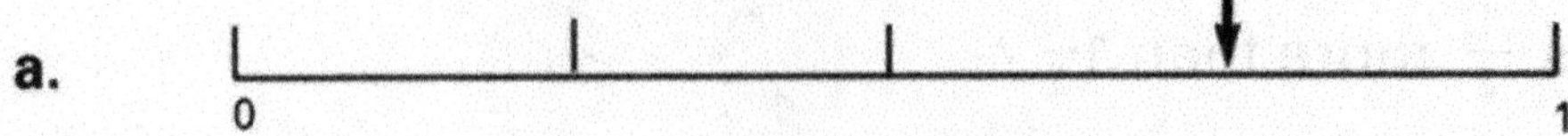

b. 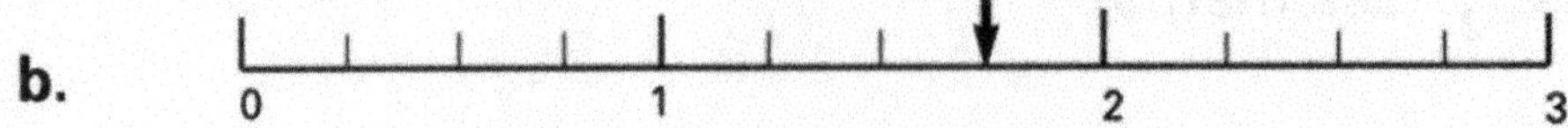

c. 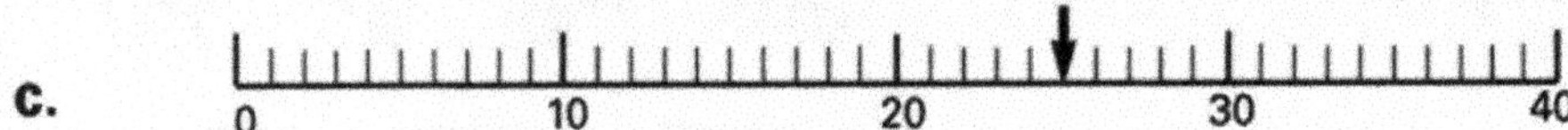

d. 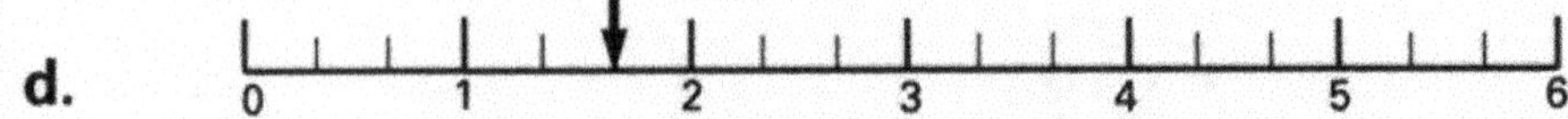

e. 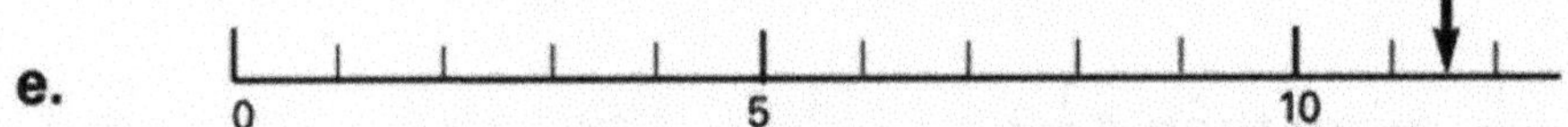

f. 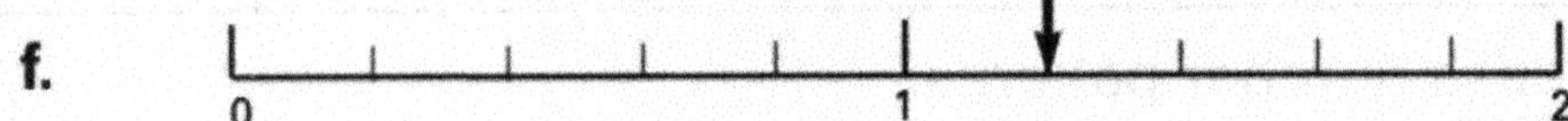

Draw these number lines in your exercise book and put in the missing numbers.

1. 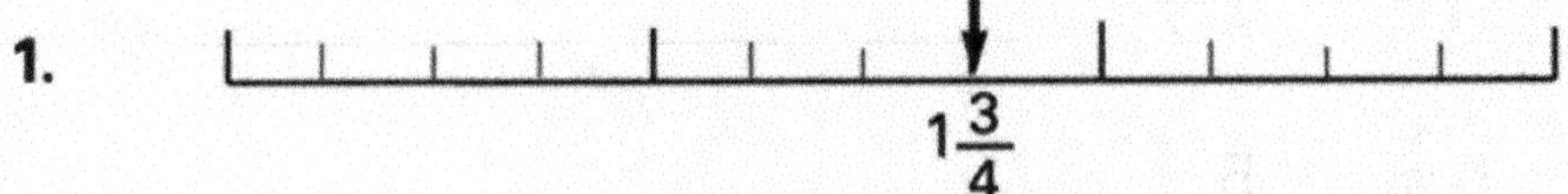

2. 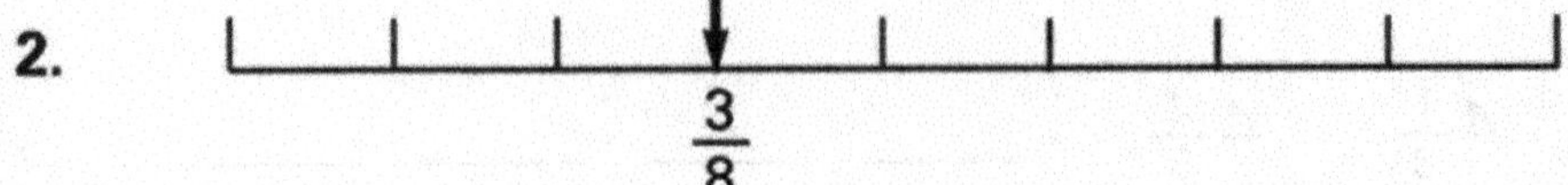

3. 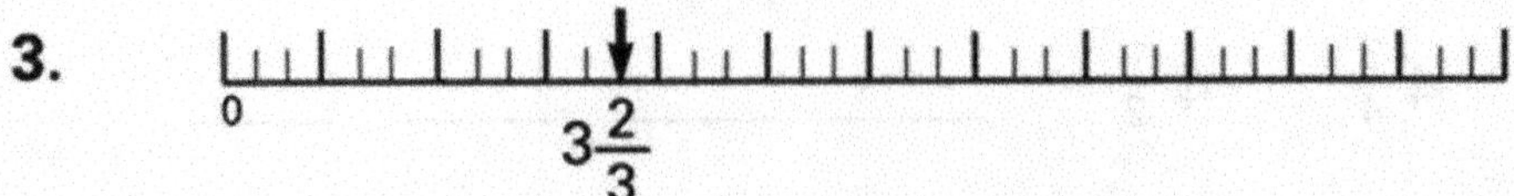

What fraction is marked on each number line? Write the answers in your exercise book.

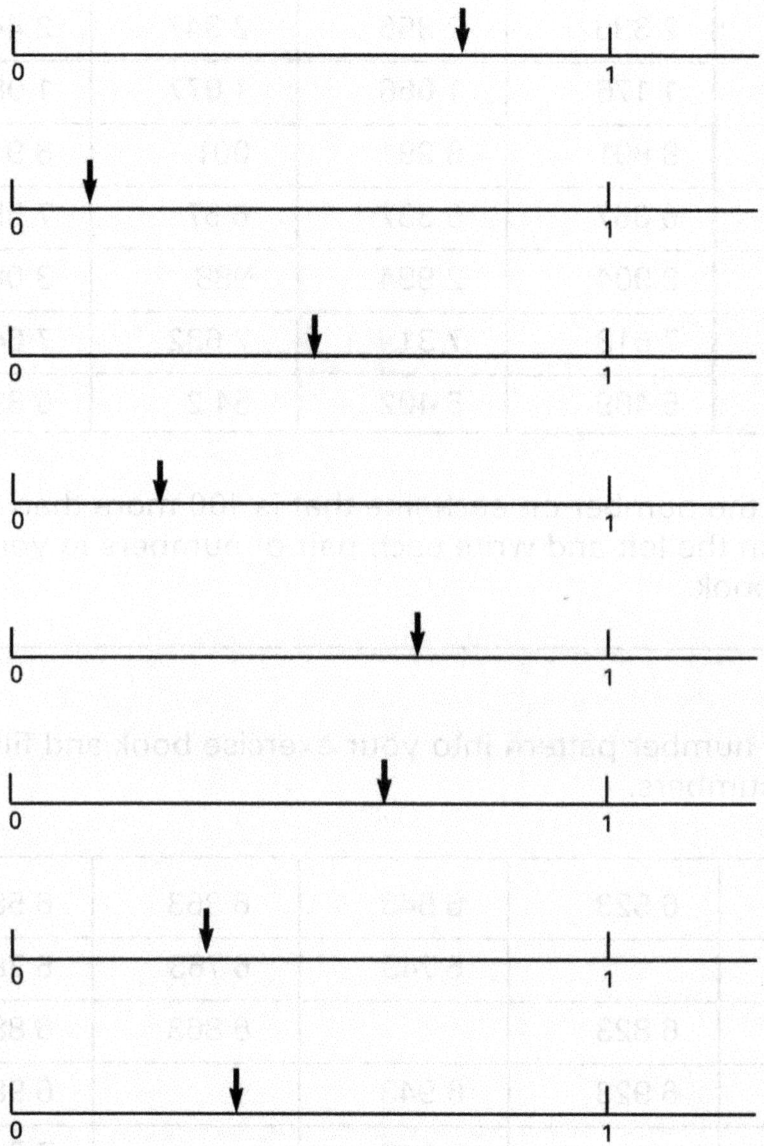

On each line, find the number that is 10 more than the number on the left in the shaded area. Write each pair of numbers in your exercise book.

2 346	2 336	2 356	2 347	2 446
1 076	1 176	1 066	1 077	1 086
8 901	8 801	8 991	001	8 911
6 357	6 367	6 337	6 57	7 557
2 984	2 904	2 994	988	3 084
7 631	7 613	7 31	7 632	7 641
5 392	5 409	5 402	54 2	5 393

Now find the number on each line that is 100 more than the number on the left and write each pair of numbers in your exercise book.

Copy this number pattern into your exercise book and fill in the missing numbers.

6 503	6 523	6 543	6 363	6 583
6 603		6 743	6 763	6 783
	6 823		6 863	6 883
6 903	6 923	6 943		6 983
7 003		7 043		7 083
7 103	7 123		7 163	

In your exercise book, write how much money is shown altogether in each box.

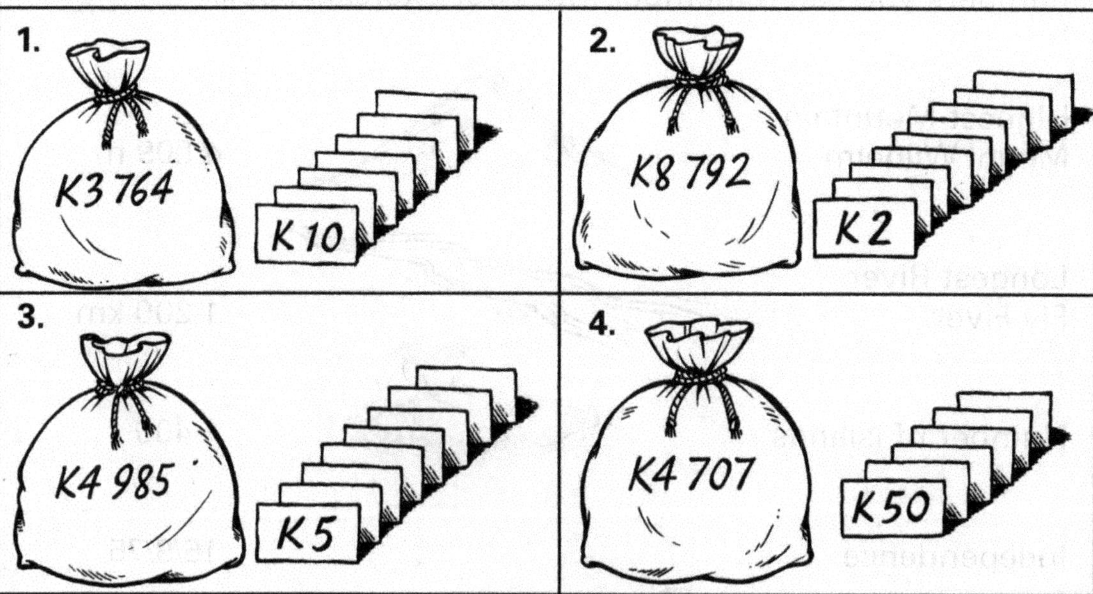

Copy these number patterns into your exercise book and write in the missing numbers.

a.	4 762	4 760	______	______	______
b.	______	9 832	9 822	______	______
c.	______	______	2 346	2 351	______
d.	______	8 506	8 516	______	______

Make up your own counting patterns starting and finishing with these numbers. Write your patterns in your exercise book.

3 762 .... 3 812

8 413 .... 8 388

Here are some facts about Papua New Guinea. Look at these numbers for one minute then close this book. Write all the numbers you can remember into your exercise book.

Highest Mountain
Mount Wilhelm — 4 509 m

Longest River
Fly Fiver — 1 200 km

Number of islands — 1 400

Independence — 16/9/75

700 different types of

179 different types of

33 different types of

13 different types of

2 300 different types of

195 different types of

300 different types of

8 different types of

Copy this table into your exercise book and fill in the empty boxes so that each pattern has a matching rule.	
211, 216, 221, 226, 231 . . . adding on 5	Start at 211 and keep adding on 5
	Put two circles after each triangle
	Start at 99 and keep taking away 2
	Start at 11 and keep adding 10
9, 18, 27, 36, 45, 54 . . .	
80, 76, 72, 68, 64, 60 . . .	
	Start at 1.00 and keep adding half hours.
$\frac{1}{4}$ $\frac{2}{4}$ $\frac{3}{4}$ 1 $1\frac{1}{4}$ $1\frac{2}{4}$ $1\frac{3}{4}$	
Now make up a pattern of your own and write it into your exercise book. Ask a friend to write the rule for your pattern.	

In your exercise book, write the answers to these questions.

1. It is 26° at 8.00 a.m. It gets 1° hotter every hour. What is the temperature at:
   11.00 a.m.
   1.00 p.m.
   3.00 p.m.?

2. Pineapple plants need to be planted 1 m apart. How long would the row be if we planted:
   2 plants
   4 plants
   15 plants?

3. There were 8 people at the bus stop at 9.00 a.m. One more person came every minute. How many people were there at:
   9.01 a.m.
   9.03 a.m.
   9.10 a.m.?

4. Joshua was 75 cm tall on his second birthday. If he grew 4 cm per year, how tall would he be when he turned:
   3 years old
   4 years old
   6 years old

5. I had 26 mangoes at my market stall. I sold 4 every hour. How many did I have left after:
   1 hour
   3 hours
   6 hours?

6. At 9.00 a.m. I started reading at page 11 and I read 40 pages every hour. What page was I up to at:
   11.00 a.m.
   1.00 p.m.
   3.00 p.m.?

7. Make up a story of your own, like the ones above, and write it in your exercise book. Ask a friend to work out the answer.

Copy these sums into your exercise book. Use your fraction squares to help you work out the answer. The first one is done for you.

1 $\frac{5}{8} + \frac{2}{8} = \frac{7}{8}$

2. $\frac{2}{4} + \frac{1}{4} =$

3. $1\frac{1}{2} + \frac{1}{2} =$

4. $\frac{3}{8} + \frac{2}{8} =$

5. $2\frac{1}{2} + \frac{1}{2} =$

6. $1\frac{1}{8} + \frac{5}{8} =$

7. $1\frac{1}{4} + \frac{3}{4} =$

8. $2\frac{1}{4} + \frac{1}{4} =$

9. $1\frac{1}{4} + \frac{1}{4} =$

10. $\frac{1}{4} + \frac{2}{8} =$

11. $\frac{3}{4} + 2\frac{1}{2} =$

12. $\frac{5}{8} + \frac{2}{4} =$

13. $1\frac{1}{4} + 1\frac{1}{4} =$

14. $1\frac{3}{8} + \frac{1}{4} =$

15. $2\frac{1}{4} + \frac{1}{8} =$

16. $1\frac{1}{8} + \frac{3}{4} =$

Copy these sums into your exercise book. Use your fraction squares to help you work out the answer.

1. $2\frac{3}{4} - \frac{1}{4} =$

2. $1\frac{3}{8} - \frac{2}{8} =$

3. $1 - \frac{3}{4} =$

4. $2 - \frac{3}{8} =$

5. $1\frac{7}{8} - \frac{5}{8} =$

6. $1\frac{1}{4} - \frac{2}{4} =$

7. $2\frac{5}{8} - \frac{3}{8} =$

8. $1\frac{2}{4} - \frac{3}{4} =$

9. $2 - \frac{1}{2} =$

10. $2\frac{1}{2} - \frac{3}{4} =$

11. $1\frac{3}{4} - \frac{1}{2} =$

12. $2 - \frac{7}{8} =$

13. $1\frac{7}{8} - 1\frac{3}{4} =$

14. $1\frac{1}{4} - 1 =$

15. $2\frac{3}{4} - \frac{3}{8} =$

16. $2 - 1\frac{1}{4} =$

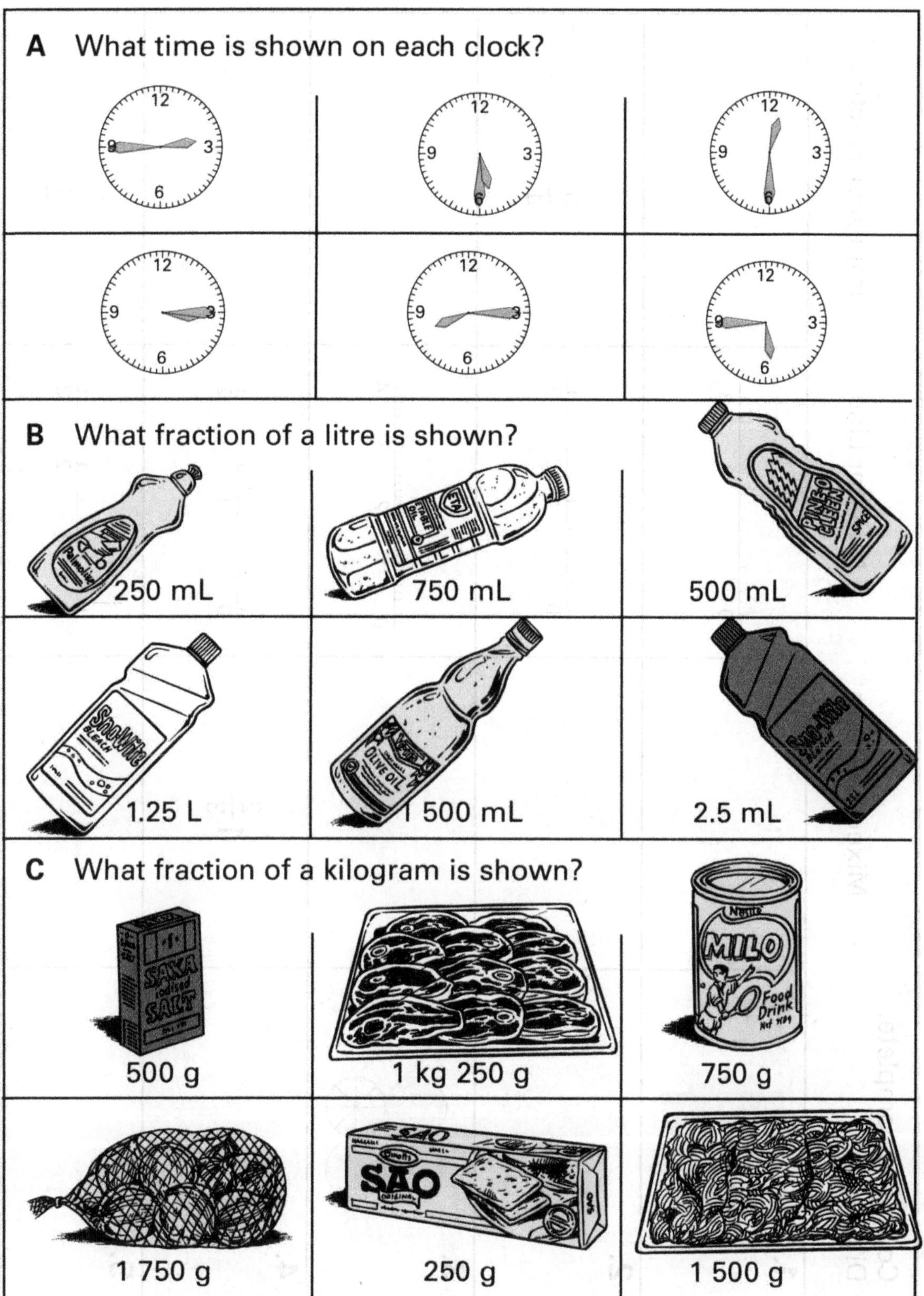
A What time is shown on each clock?
12
9
3
6
B What fraction of a litre is shown?
250 mL
750 mL
500 mL
1.25 L
1 500 mL
2.5 mL
C What fraction of a kilogram is shown?
SAXA
iodised
SALT
MILO
Food
Drink
SAO
500 g
1 kg 250 g
750 g
1 750 g
250 g
1 500 g

Copy and complete.

Diagram	Mixed Number	Number Line	Improper Fraction
1. 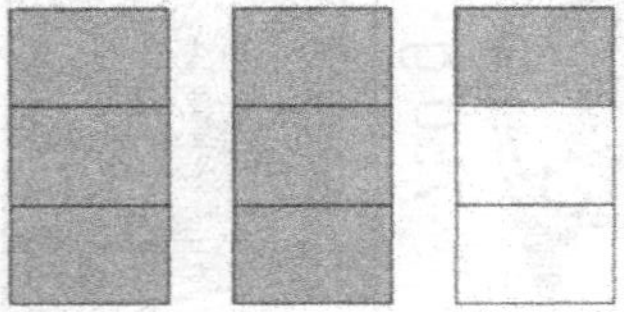		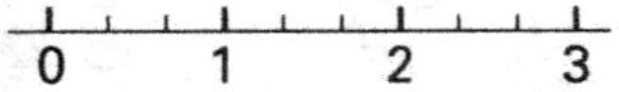 0 1 2 3	
2.		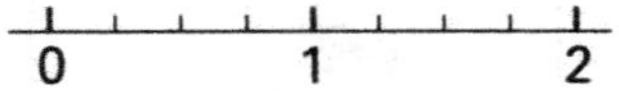 0 1 2	$\frac{5}{4}$
3. 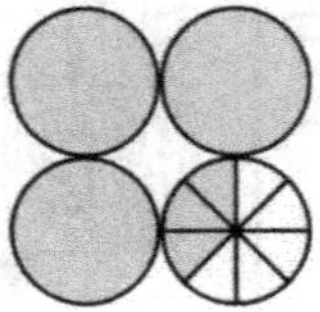		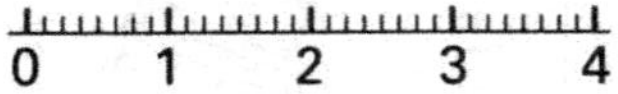 0 1 2 3 4	
4.	$1\frac{2}{3}$	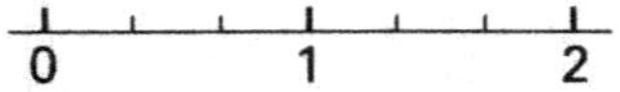 0 1 2	
5.		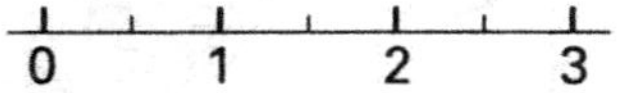 0 1 2 3	$\frac{5}{2}$

Copy these diagrams into your exercise book and beside each one write how much is shaded. Write the shaded part in two ways. The first one is done for you.

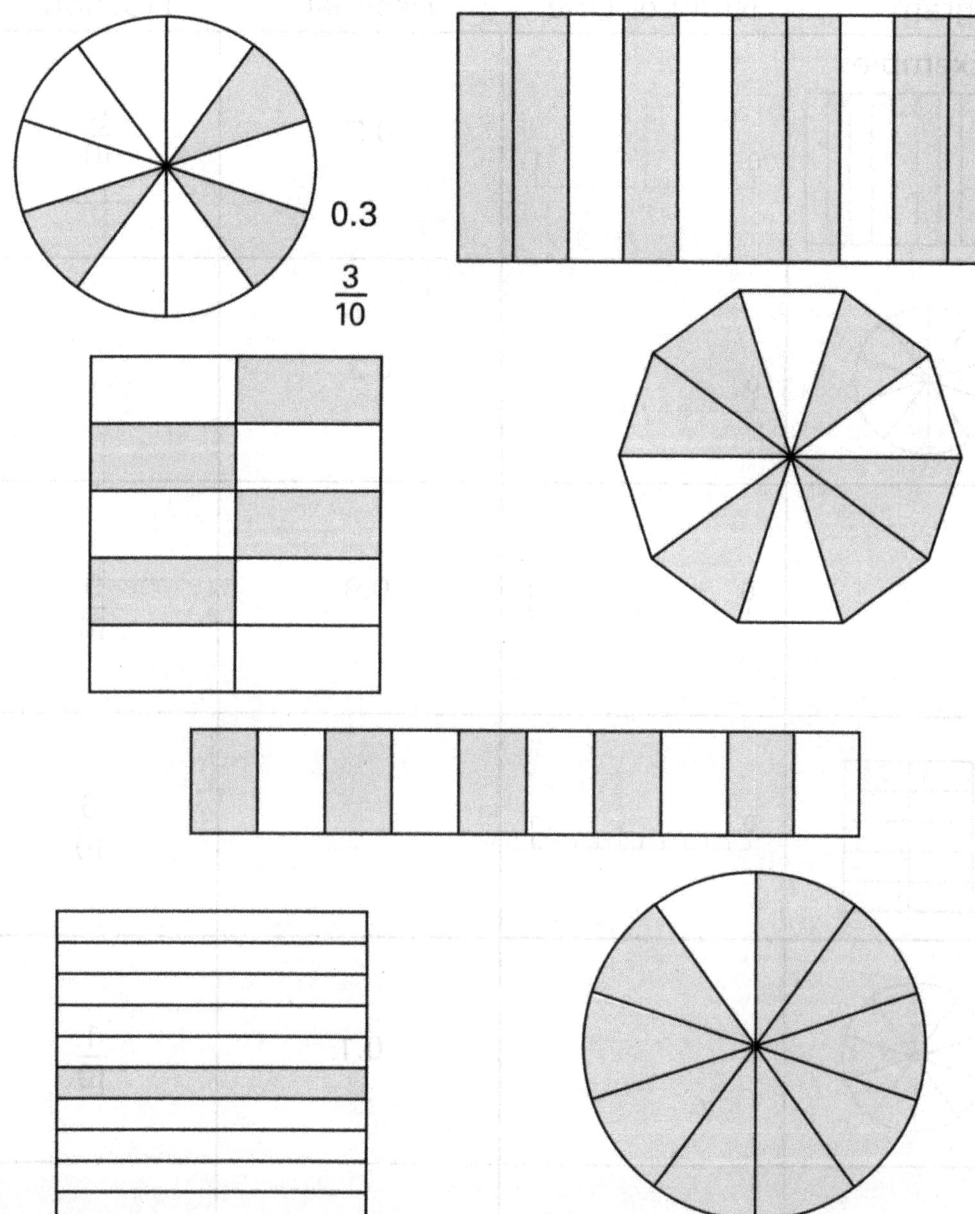

Now write how much of each diagram is not shaded. Write it in two ways.

In your exercise book complete the gaps in the table. The first one is done for you.

Diagram	Number Line	Decimal	Fraction
1. Example	0 1	0.5	$\frac{5}{10}$
2.	0 1	0.2	
3.	0 1	0.9	$\frac{9}{10}$
4.	0 1		$\frac{6}{10}$
5.		0.1	$\frac{1}{10}$
6.	0 1	0.8	$\frac{8}{10}$

What temperature is shown on these thermometers?

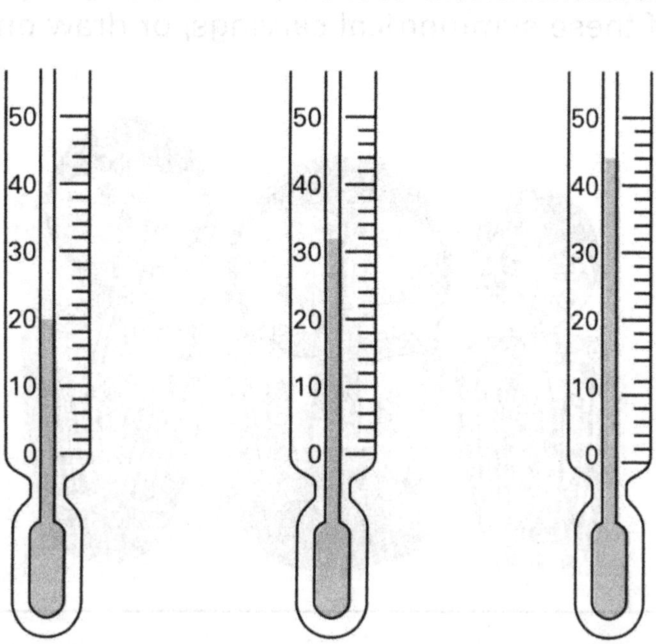

Copy these thermometers into your exercise book, and show the correct temperature.

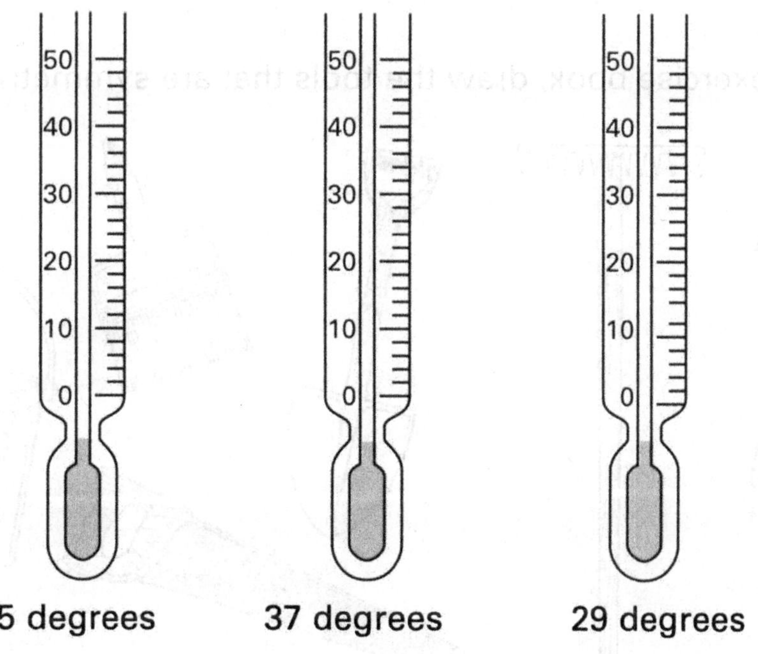

15 degrees 37 degrees 29 degrees

A
Draw one of these symmetrical carvings, or draw one of your own.

B
Draw all the capital letters of the alphabet that are symmetrical.

C
In your exercise book, draw the tools that are symmetrical.

School Garden Plan

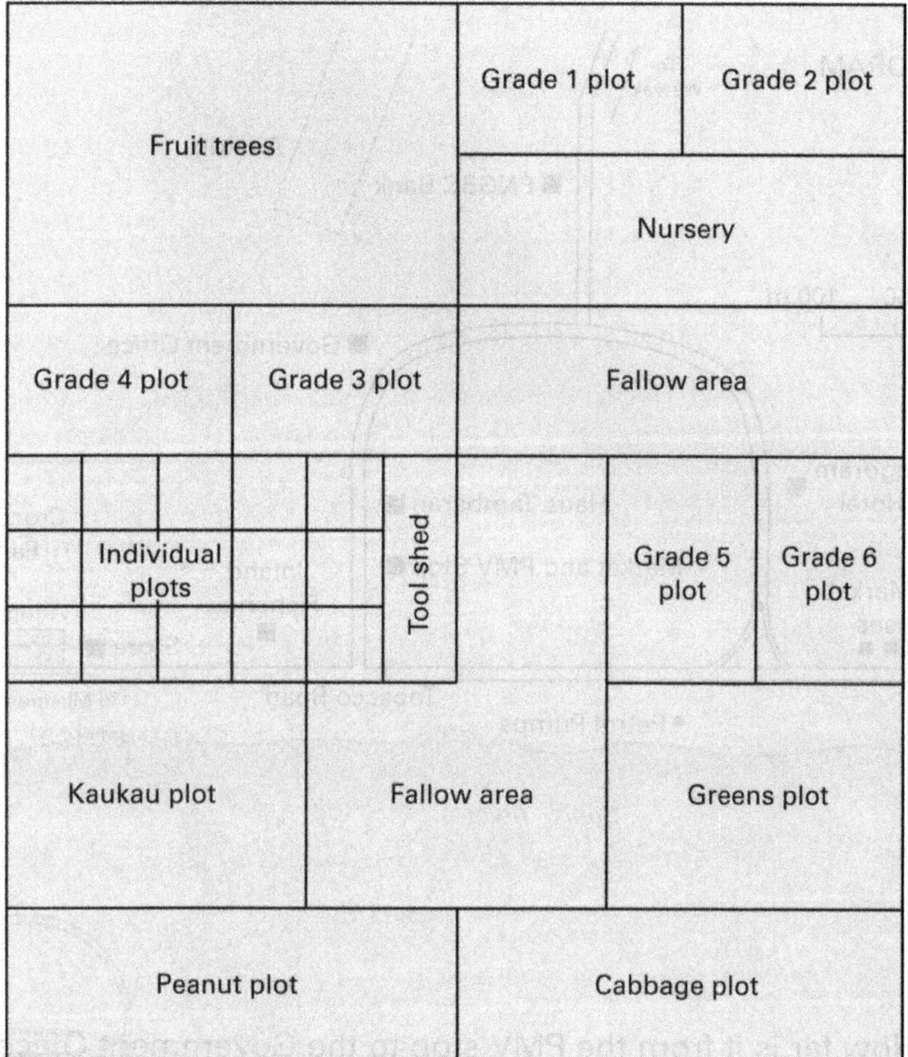

Scale: 1 cm represents 10 metres

Use the scale to work out how big each plot is.

Use the scale to help you find the distances between the main landmarks on the map.

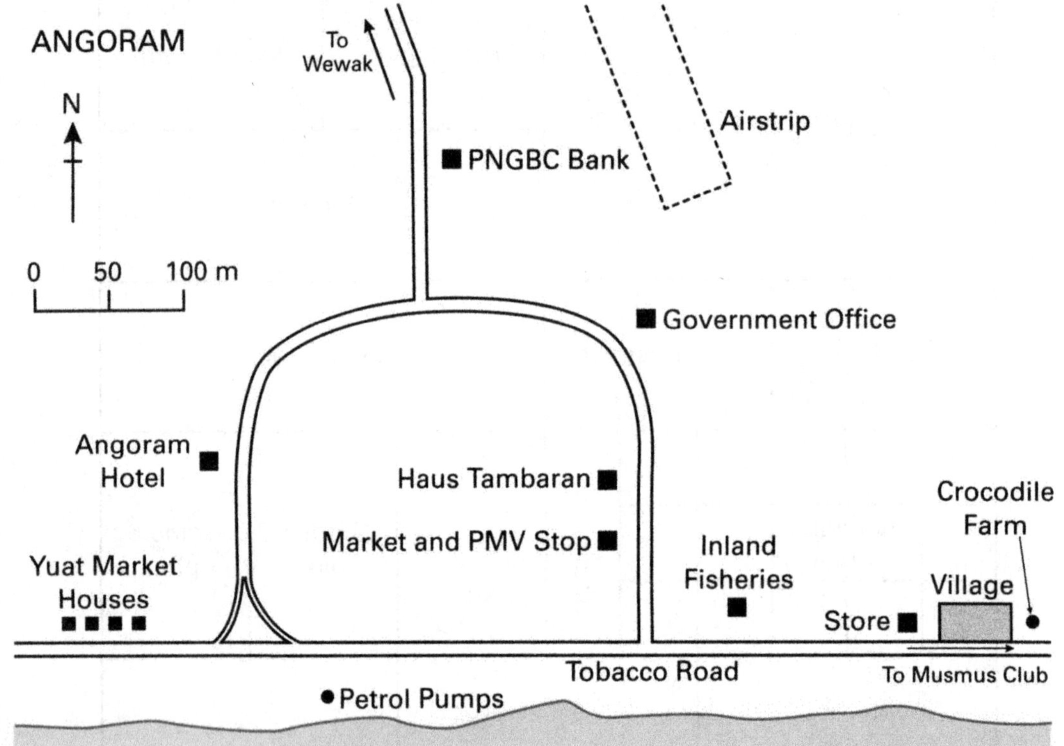

1. How far is it from the PMV stop to the Government Office?
2. How far is it from the market to the hotel?
3. How far is it from the petrol pump to the store?
4. How far is it from the market to the village?

Use the scale to find the distances between the main landmarks on the map.

Map of National Capital District

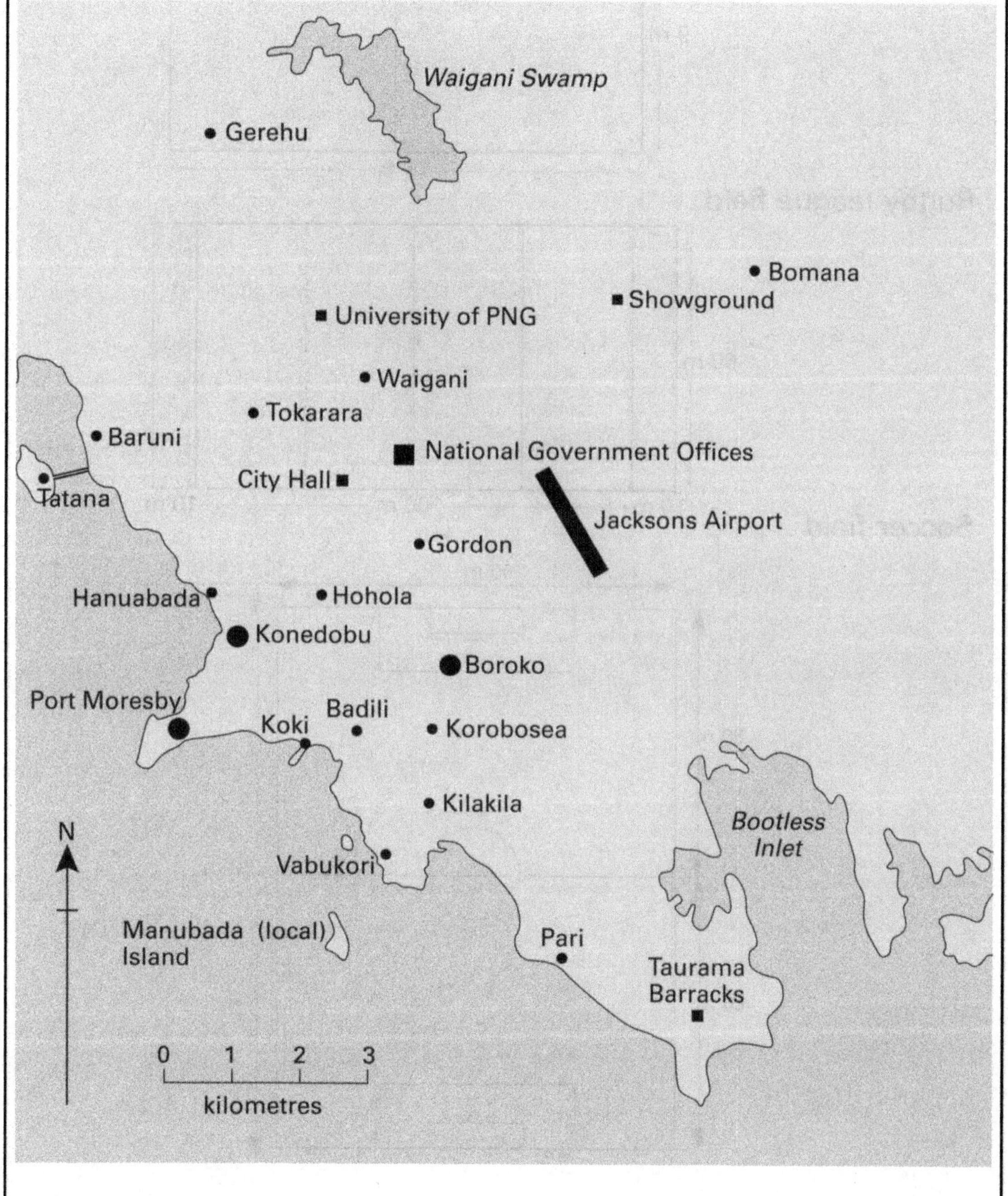

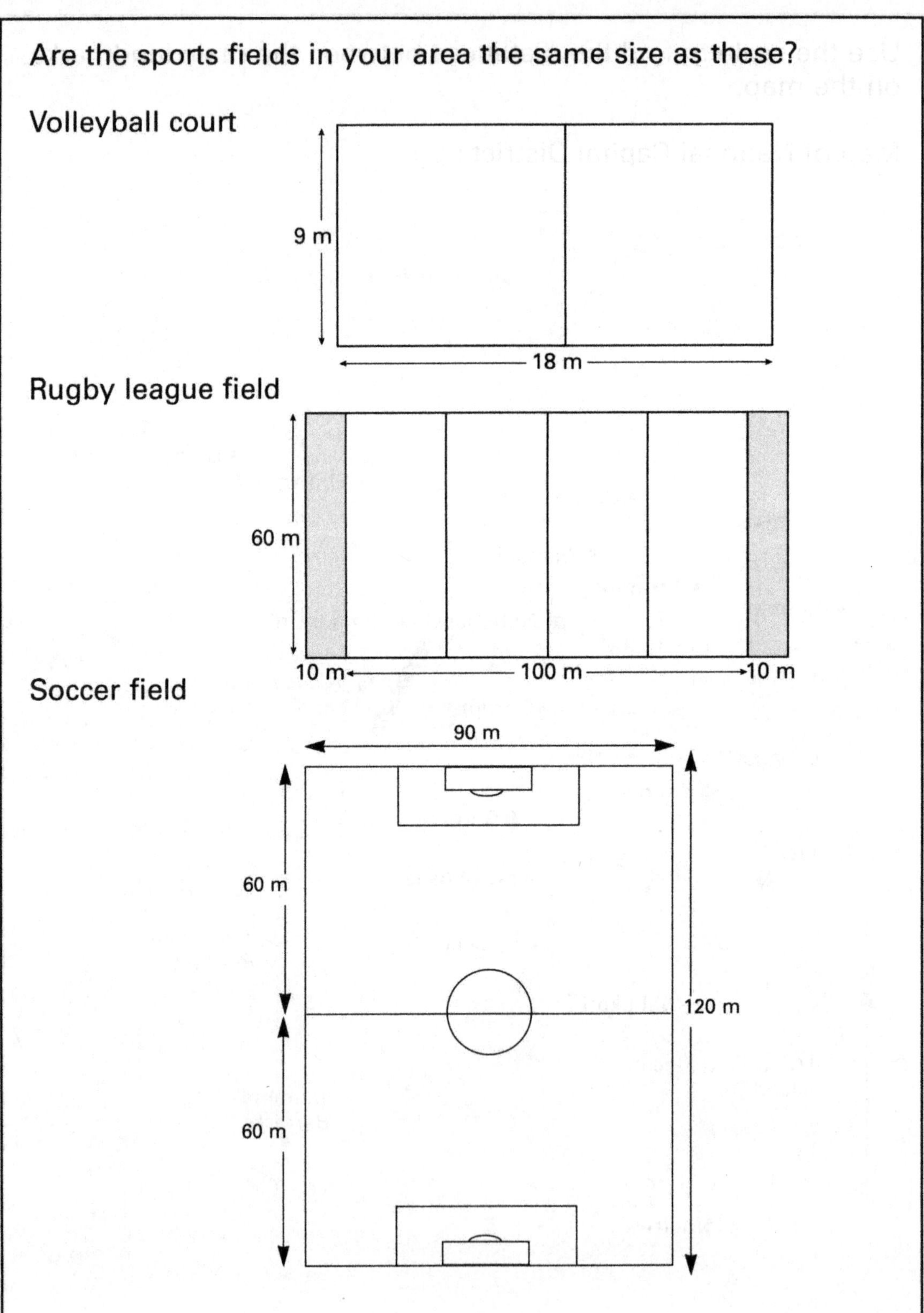
Are the sports fields in your area the same size as these?
Volleyball court
9 m
18 m
Rugby league field
60 m
10 m
100 m
10 m
Soccer field
90 m
60 m
60 m
120 m

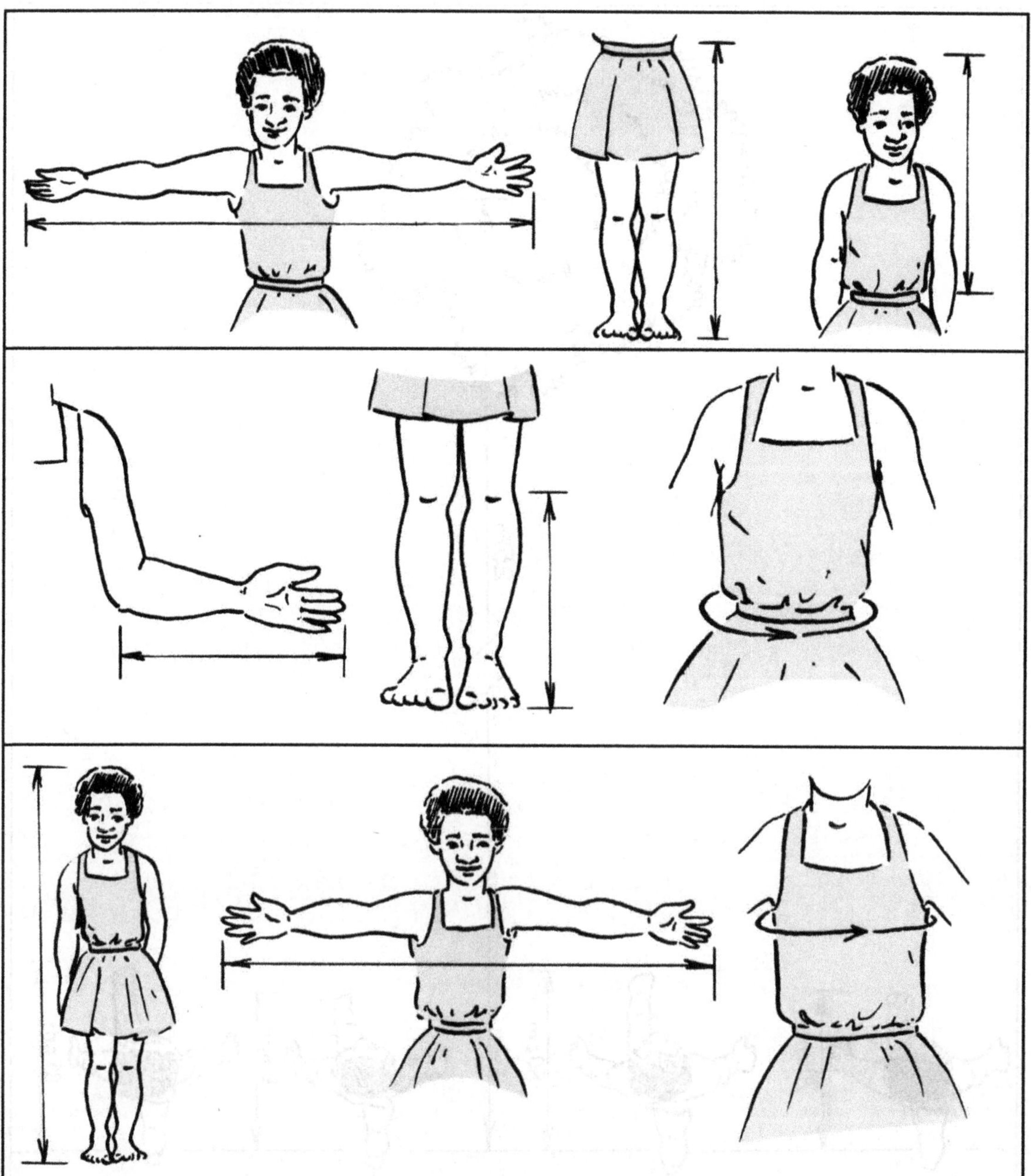

Using your body measurements, calculate:

1. How much larger is your chest than your waist?
2. If your waist is the midpoint of your height?
3. How much greater is your armspan than your waist?

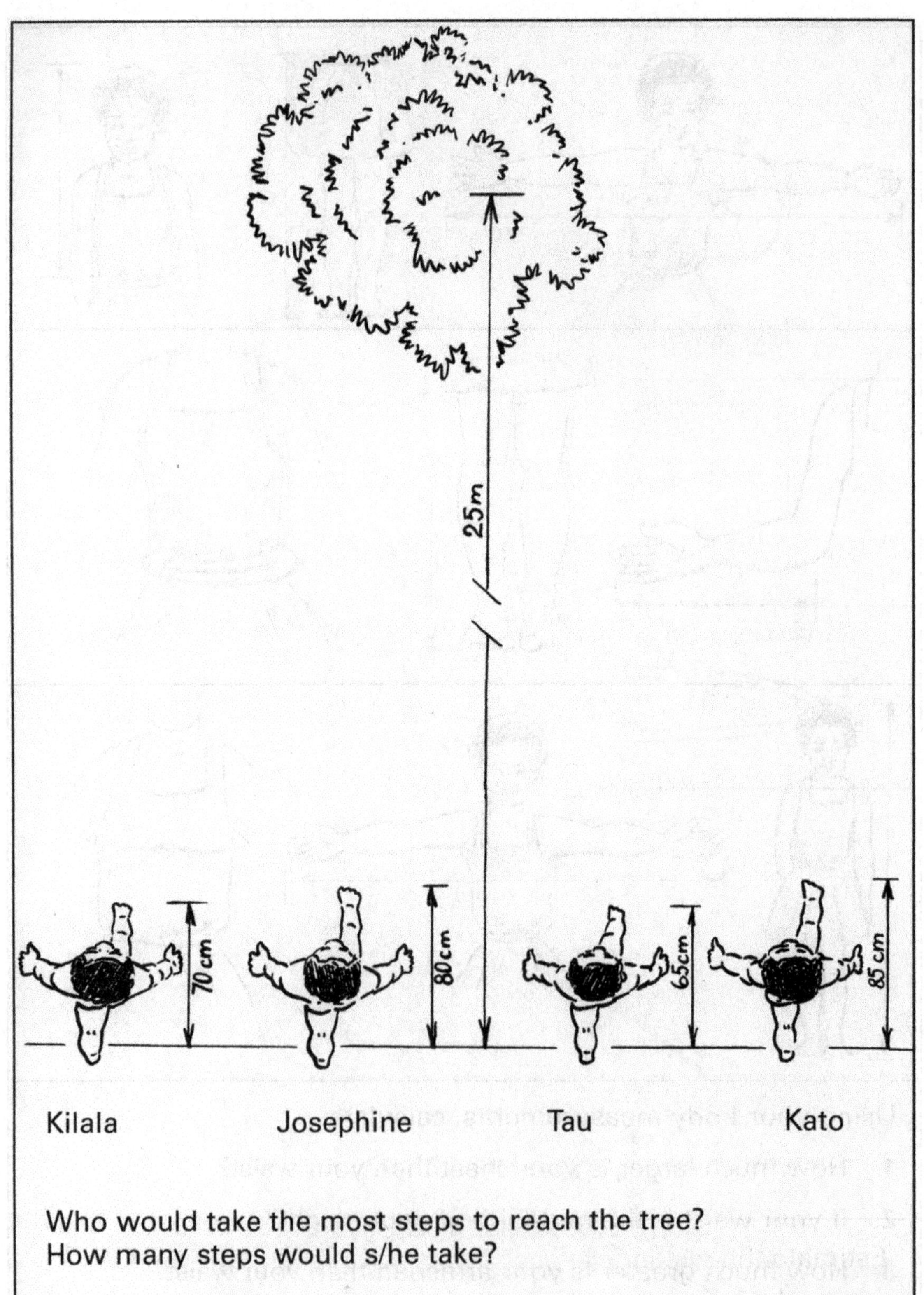
25m
70 cm
80cm
65cm
85 cm
Kilala
Josephine
Tau
Kato
Who would take the most steps to reach the tree?
How many steps would s/he take?

Estimate the distance of each South Pacific Games record.

In your exercise book, write how much water is in each container.

1. Which containers hold more than 500 mL?
2. Which containers hold exactly $\frac{1}{4}$ litre?
3. Which containers hold less than 250 mL?
4. Which containers hold less than 500 mL?
5. Which containers hold between 250 mL and 500 mL?

1. Find a combination of containers that would fill the 750 mL container.
2. Find a combination of containers that would fill the 1 litre container.
3. Find some other different ways to fill the 750 mL container.
4. Find some other different ways to fill the 1 L container.

1. Write the capacity of each container in millilitres.
2. Which two containers are most different in capacity?
3. Which two containers are closest together in capacity?

1. The labels on these containers show how much each one holds. Put the items above in order from the smallest to the largest volume.
2. Robert was sick and the doctor gave him a bottle of medicine. He also gave him a medicine measure. The measure held 5 mL. The doctor told Robert to take 5 mL of medicine 3 times a day for 5 days. How much medicine did Robert take each day? How much did he take in 5 days?
3. Mrs Kariko drinks six cups of tea every day. Each cup holds 300 mL. How many litres and millilitres of tea does Mrs Kariko drink in a day?
4. How much water do you drink each day?

Total the capacity of each shopping list to find which one has the greatest/smallest capacity.

Vele Family 2 L milk 1 L orange juice 750 mL cooking oil 1 250 mL bleach 2 L kerosene 250 mL cough medicine	**Uralom Family** 1 L kerosene 1 L tomato sauce 500 mL dish-washing liquid 500 mL orange juice 2 L milk 200 mL Magi sauce
Sevese Family 250 mL Detto 500 mL Pine-o-cleen 1 L Coke 2 L milk 300 mL chilli sauce 750 mL bleach	**Afito Family** 1 L milk 2 L bleach 2 L cordial 750 mL dish-washing liquid 250 mL shampoo

1. Which shape has the largest perimeter?
2. Which shape has the smallest perimeter?
3. Calculate the perimeter of each shape and write the answer in your exercise book.
4. Were your estimates correct?

a

b

c

d

e

f.

1. Calculate the perimeter of these shapes.

2. Explain the method you used to work out the answers.

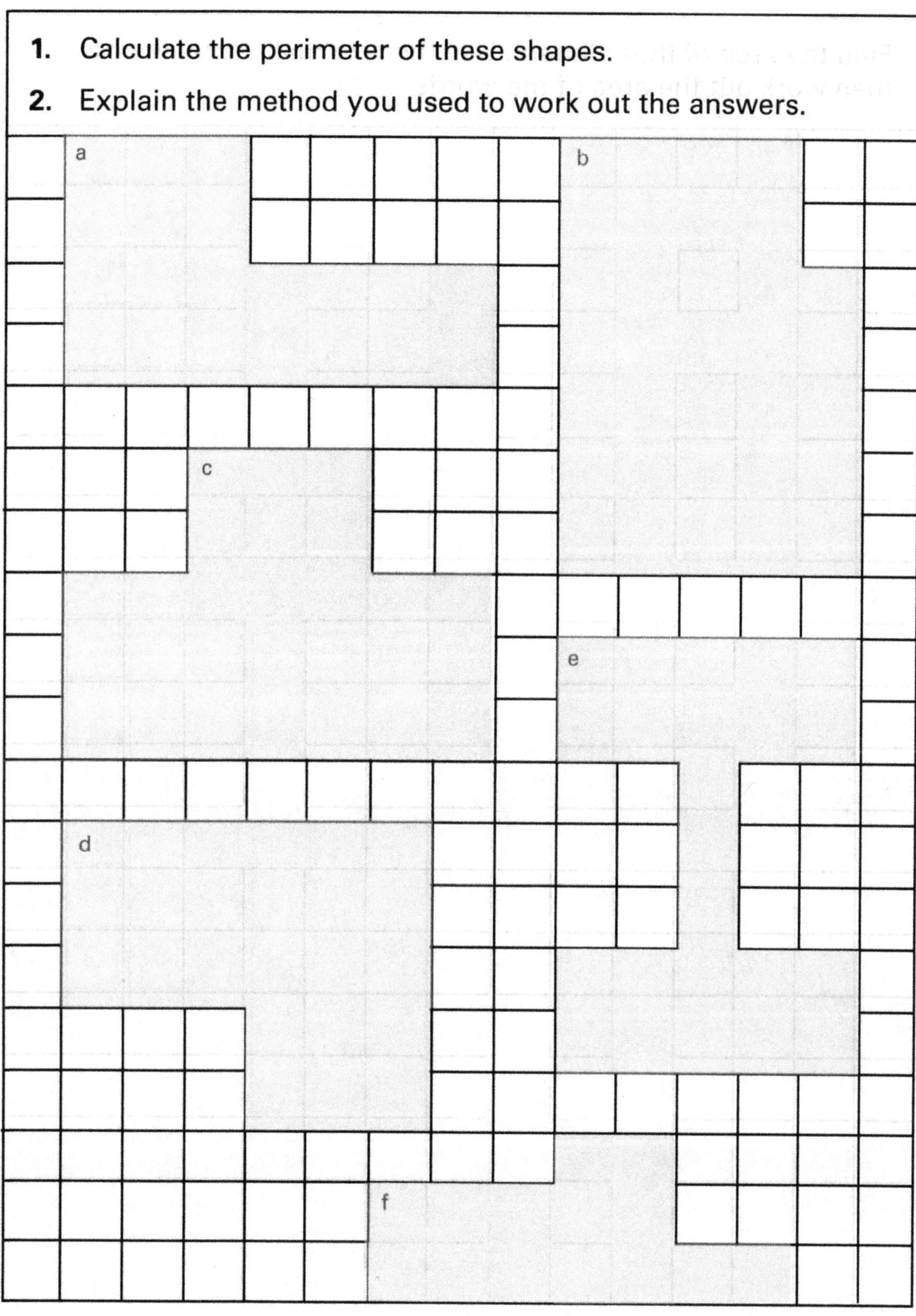

Find the area of these letters. Use them to make some words, then work out the area of the words.

Find the area of these letters. Use them and the letters on the previous page to make more words.

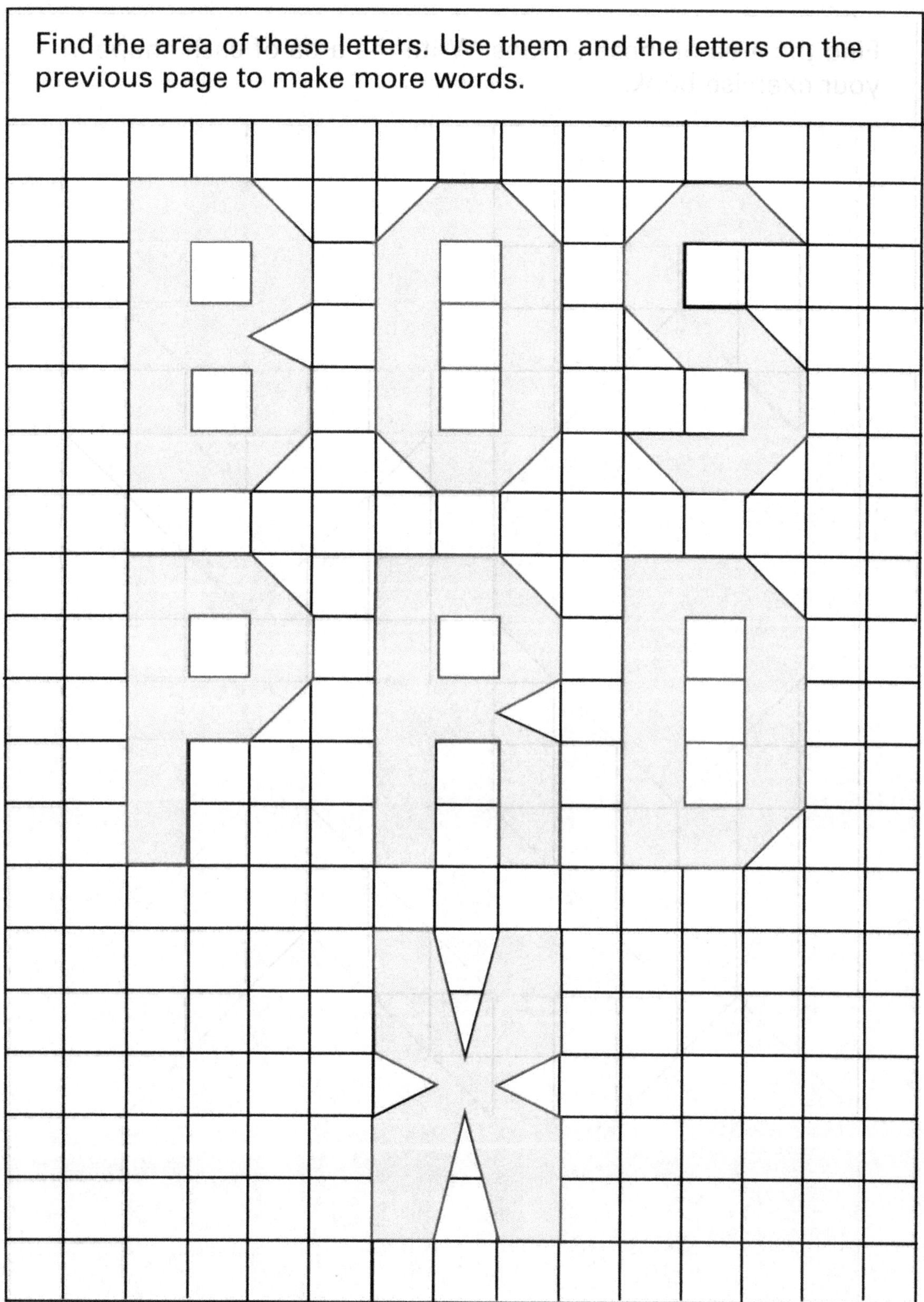

Find the area of these shapes. Write the area of each shape in your exercise book.

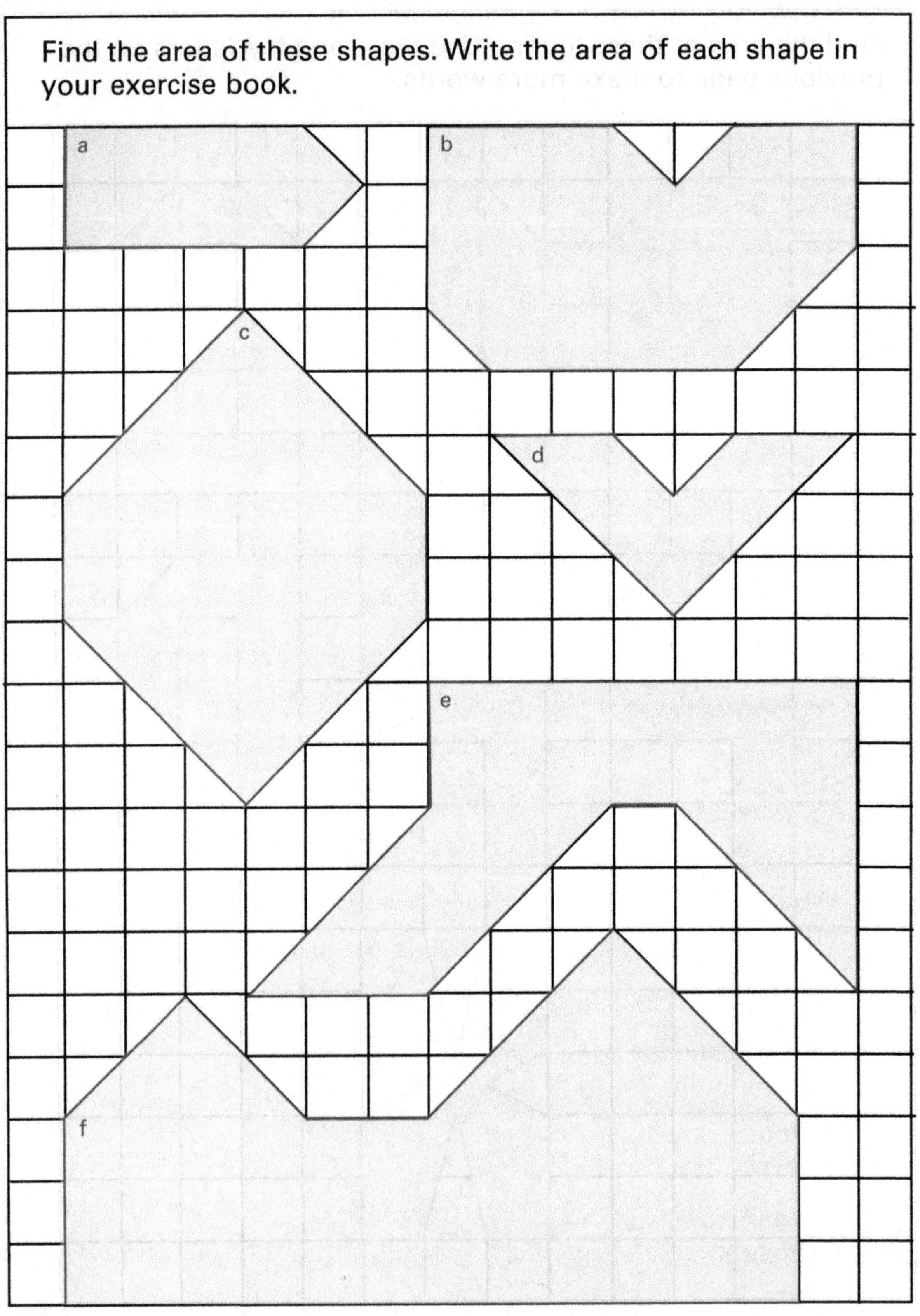

A

B

i l d r j q

s t h f c o b

a u m

g e p n v k

C

1. What is the same about all the items in:
   Frame A?
   Frame B?
   Frame C?
2. In your exercise book, copy all the fruit from Frame A, sorting it into 2 sets. Make up a name for each set.
3. In your exercise book, sort all the letters into sets, and name each set. You can make more than two sets if you like.
4. In your exercise book, sort all the transport into sets. Label your sets.

A

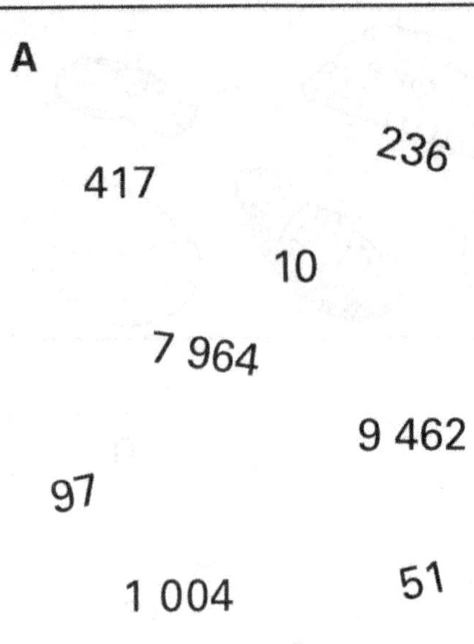

List the elements of the set of odd numbers.

B

Draw the elements of the set of triangles.

C

List the elements of the set of animals with six legs.

D

List the elements of sets of animals that live in trees.

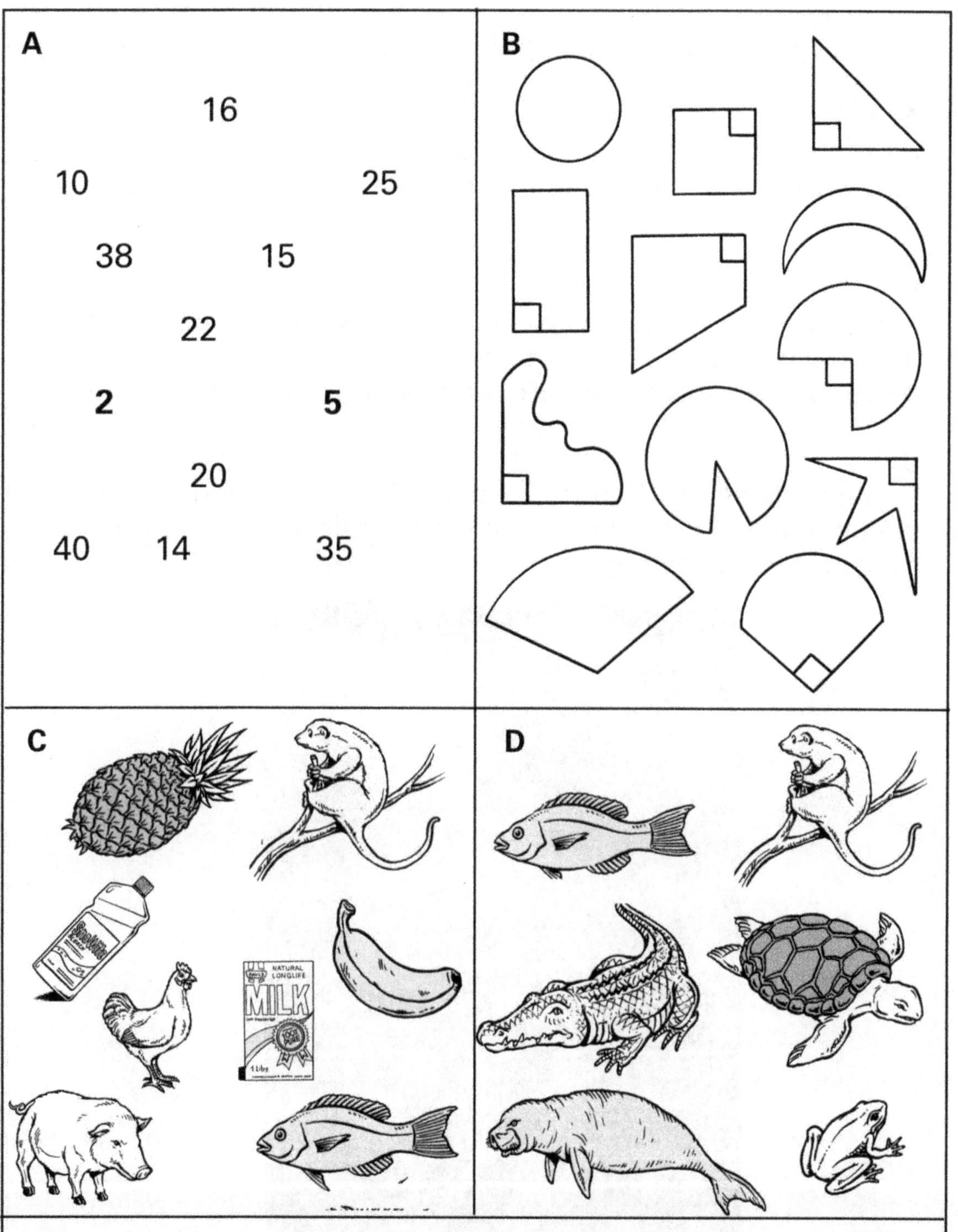

For each Frame, draw two overlapping circles and show which set each item belongs to.

Draw overlapping circles to help you solve these problems.

A

I had 12 mangoes and 10 pawpaws to share with our class of 18 children. How many children could have a mango and a pawpaw?

B

In our school garden next week, we will have ten workers. We need six people to do the weeding and six people to pick pineapples for the market. How many will have to do two jobs?

C

At the trade store, I bought six bottles of orange and six bottles of lemonade. If I share these with my family of eight people, how many will have two bottles of soft drink?

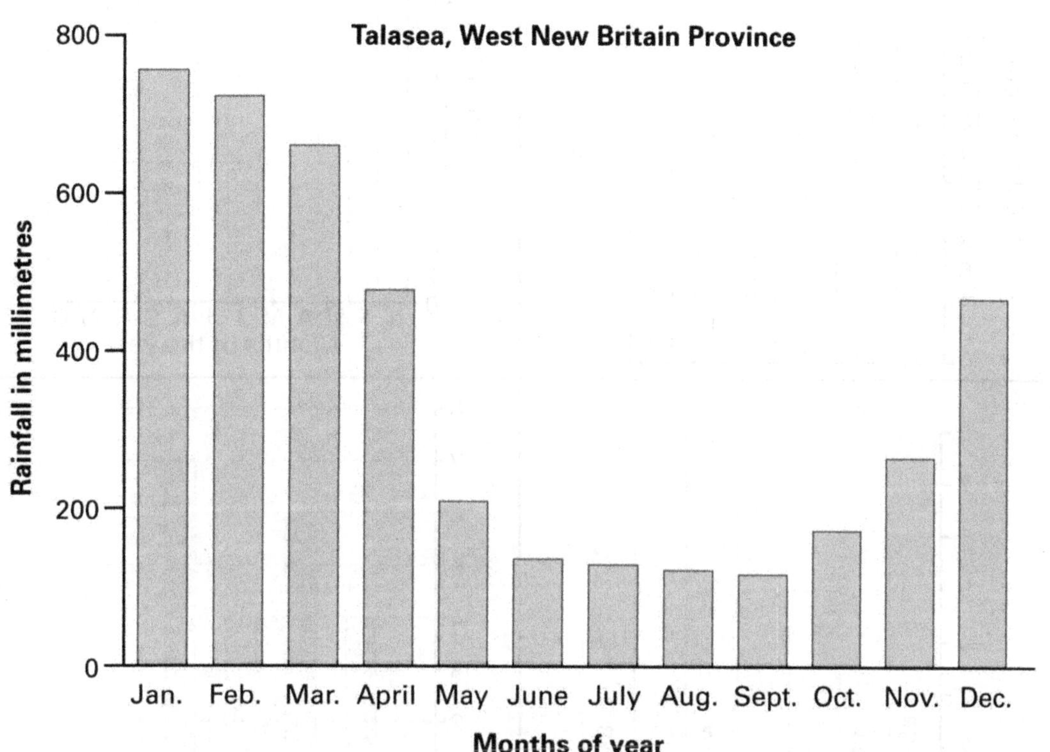

1. Which is the wettest month?
2. Which is the driest month?
3. How much more rainfall is there in January than there is in July?
4. When is the wet season?
5. How much rain falls in May?
6. Is April wetter than November?
7. What months make up the dry season?
8. Is Christmas Day likely to be rainy? Why?

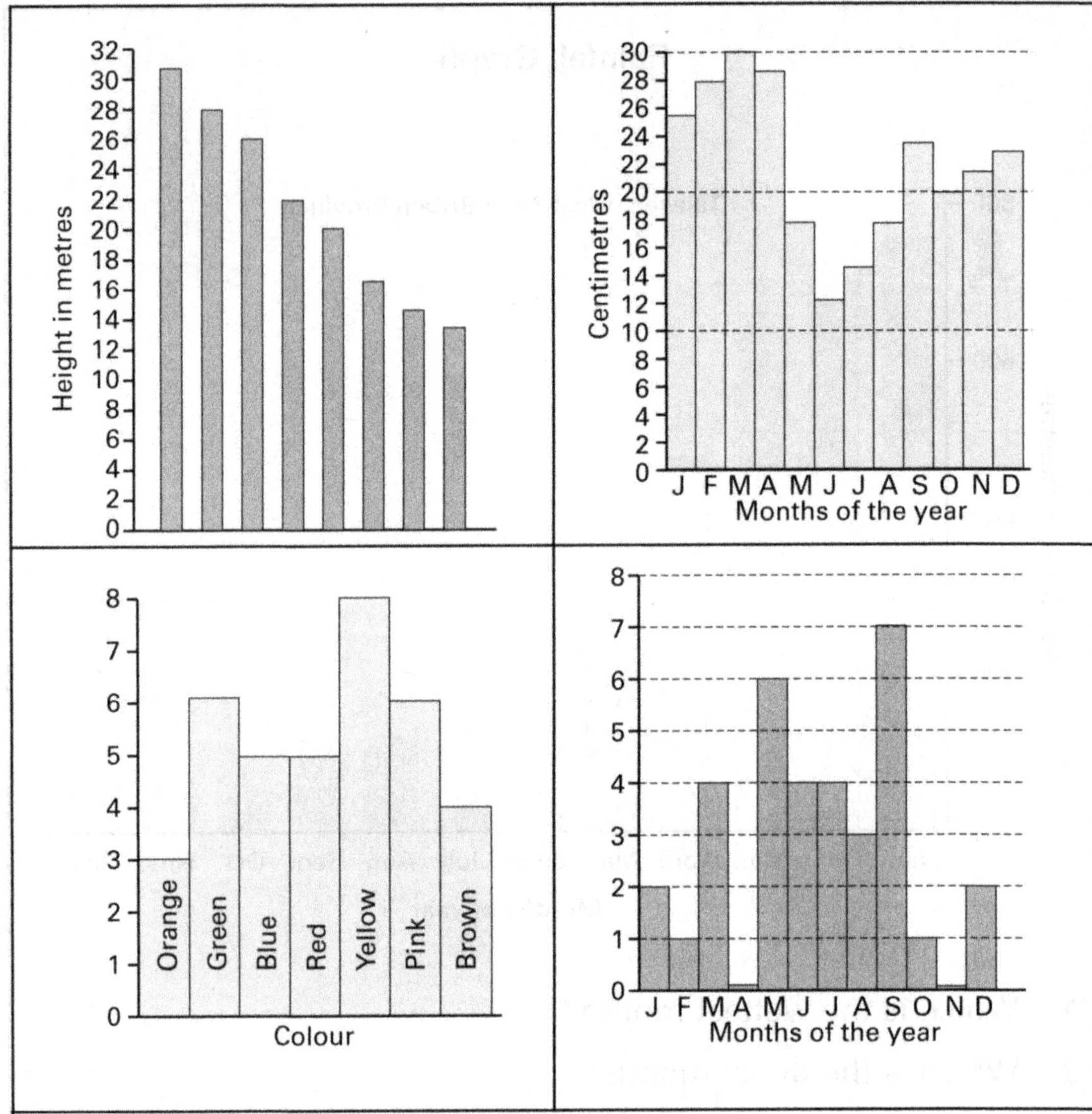

1. Look carefully at each graph and decide what it could be about.
2. Make up a title for each graph.
3. Check that labels have been put on each graph and write in any missing labels.
4. Choose one graph to copy into your exercise book. Write a story about your graph.

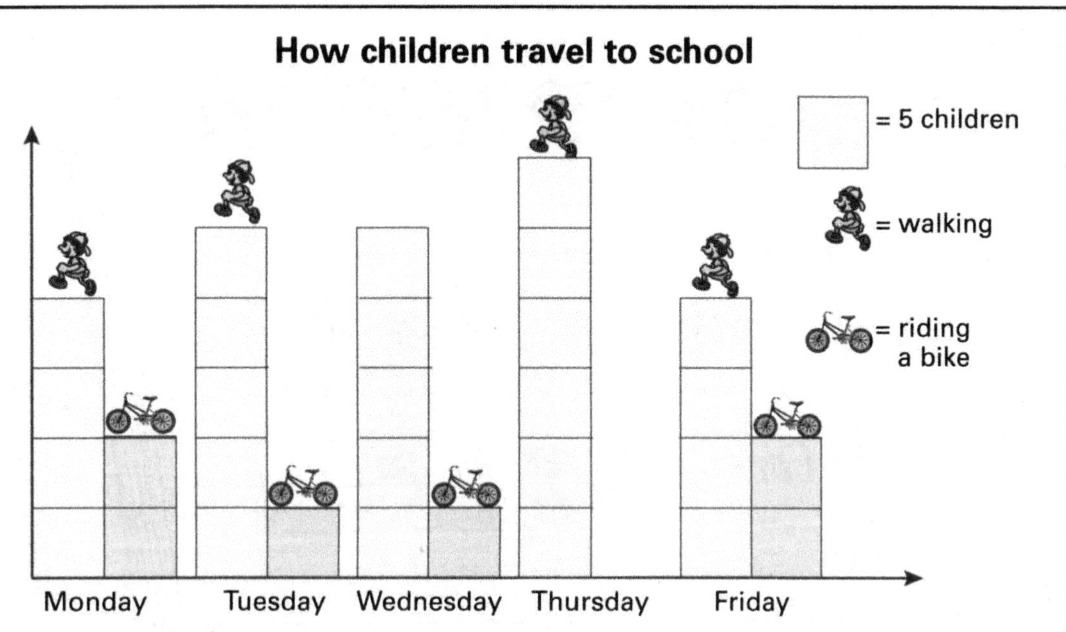

How many children took part in this survey?

How many children own bicycles? What does this graph tell us?

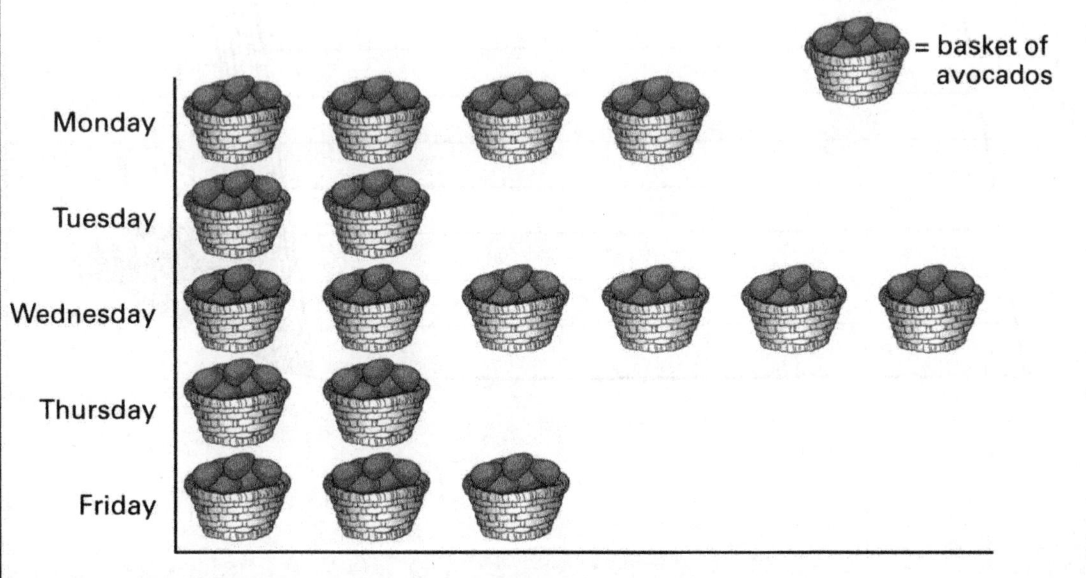

Think of a suitable name for this graph.

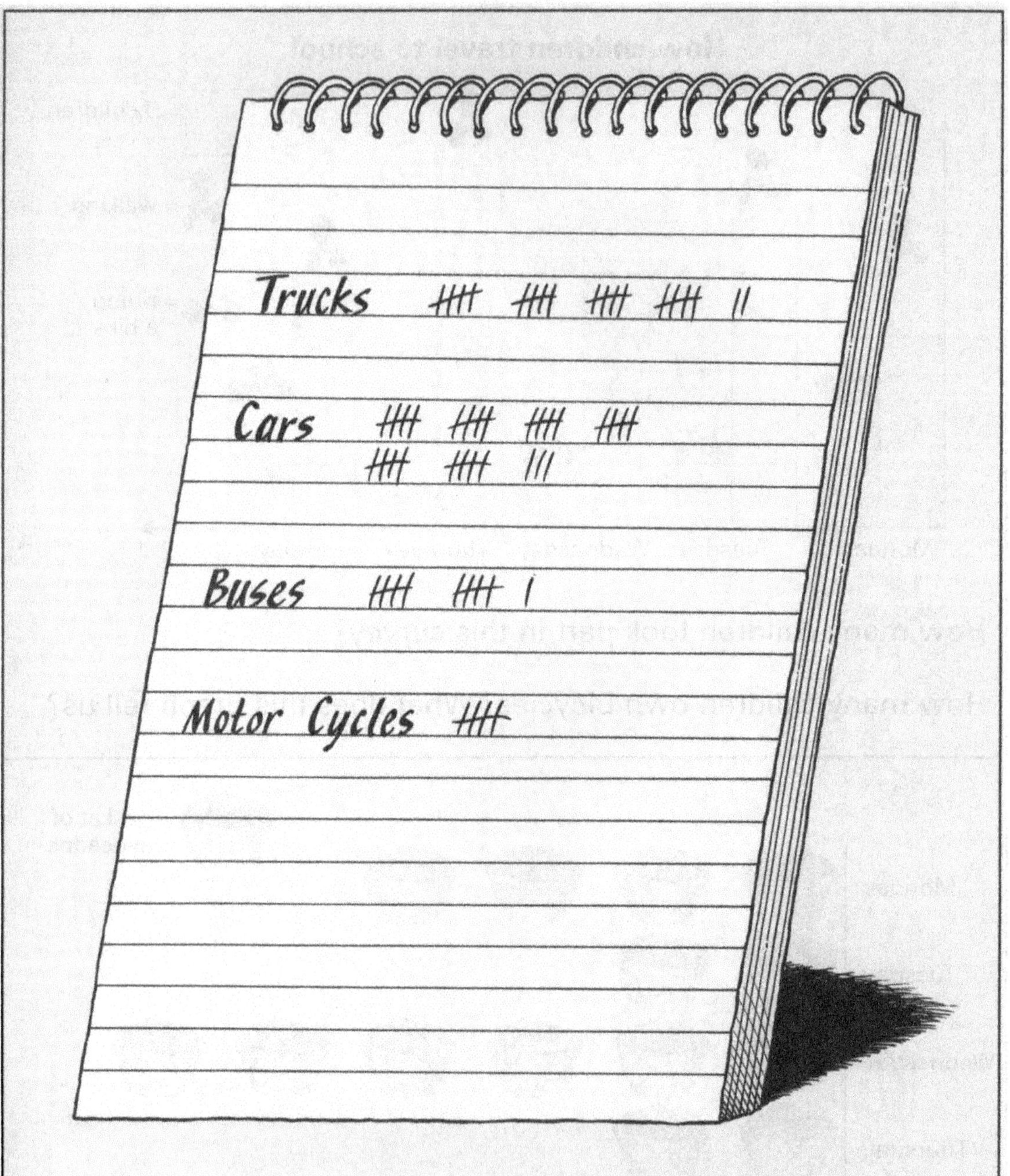

Make your own graph to represent the information shown on this chart.

Make a graph about any of the information shown in this picture.

A

B

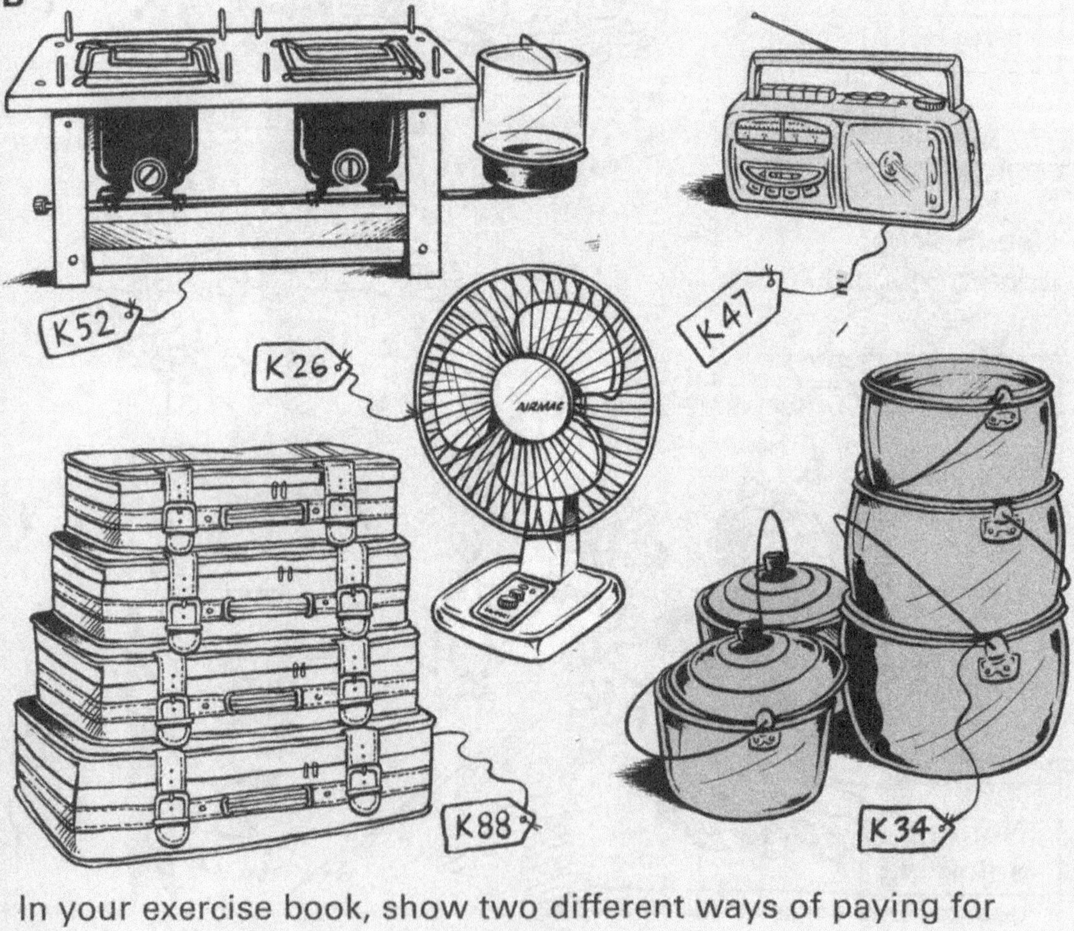

K52

K26

K47

K88

K34

In your exercise book, show two different ways of paying for each of these items.

How could you pay for these items?

A

This man is a cleaner. He works eight hours each day and gets paid K1.25 per hour. He works five days each week. Use this information to complete the chart.

Time	Wages	Time	Wages
2 hours		5 days	
4 hours		2 weeks	
1 day			K550
2 days		4 weeks 2 days	

B

Use the cost per minute shown below to help you work out the price of each STD telephone call.

Zone	cost per minute	2 min	5 min	10 min	20 min	30 min
Same call zone	25t					
Adjoining call zone	50t					
Non-adjoining call zone	75t					

Petrol 88t a litre

Diesel 54t a litre

Engine Oil K7.50 a litre

1. How much would 10 litres of petrol cost?
2. A driver pays for 10 litres of petrol and also buys 2 litres of engine oil. How much would it cost him altogether?
3. A bus driver bought $8\frac{1}{2}$ litres of diesel. How much did it cost?
4. How much would it cost to fill an 80 litre tank with diesel?
5. If a driver put 20 litres of petrol in his tank, and bought $\frac{1}{2}$ a litre of engine oil, how much would he pay altogether?
6. What would the cost of 20 litres of diesel be?
7. A driver needed engine oil. She paid K45 for it. How much engine oil did she need?
8. A car travels 10 kilometres on a litre of petrol. How much petrol would be used on a 100 kilometre trip? How much would the petrol cost?

How are these gardens different from yours?

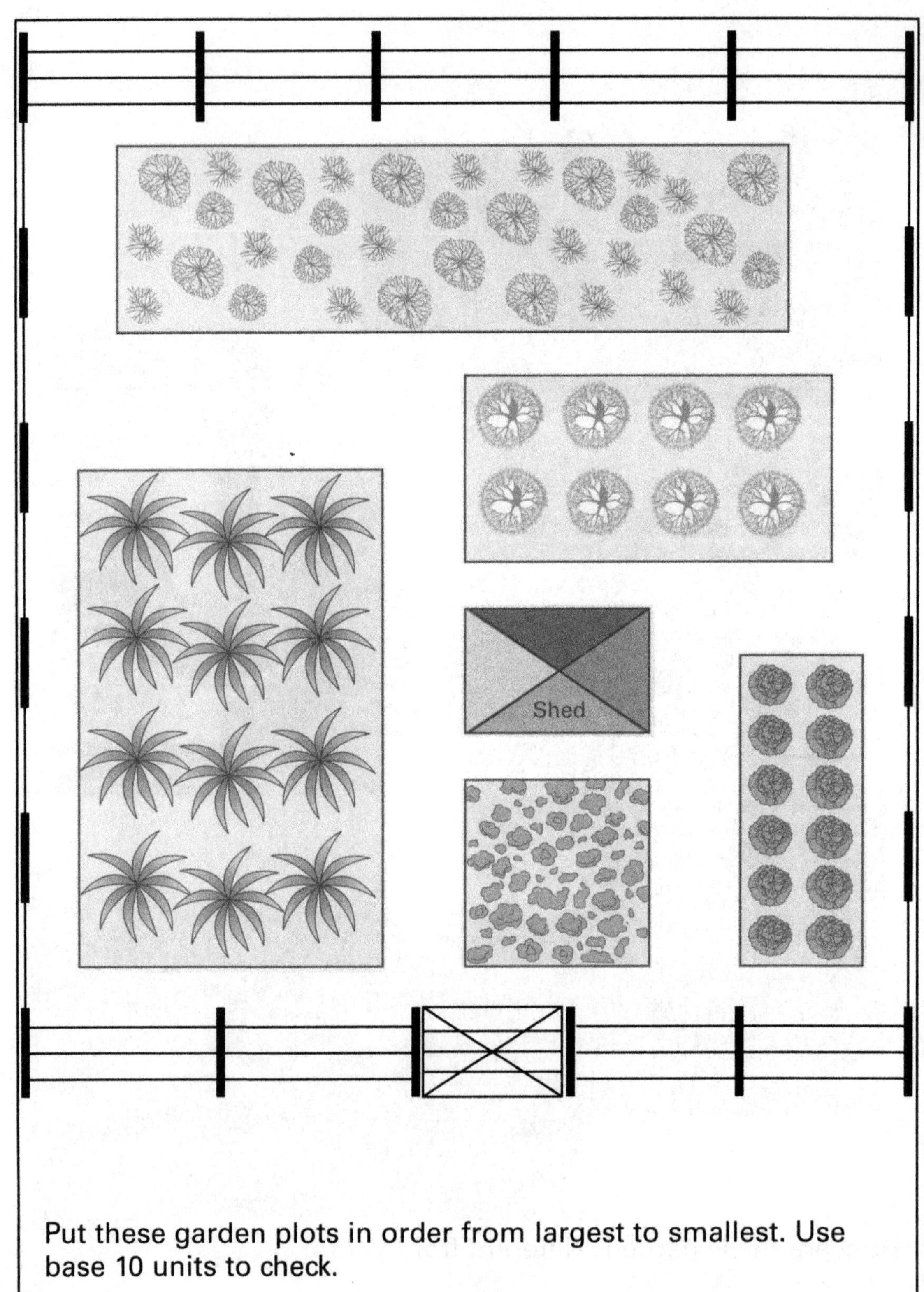

Put these garden plots in order from largest to smallest. Use base 10 units to check.

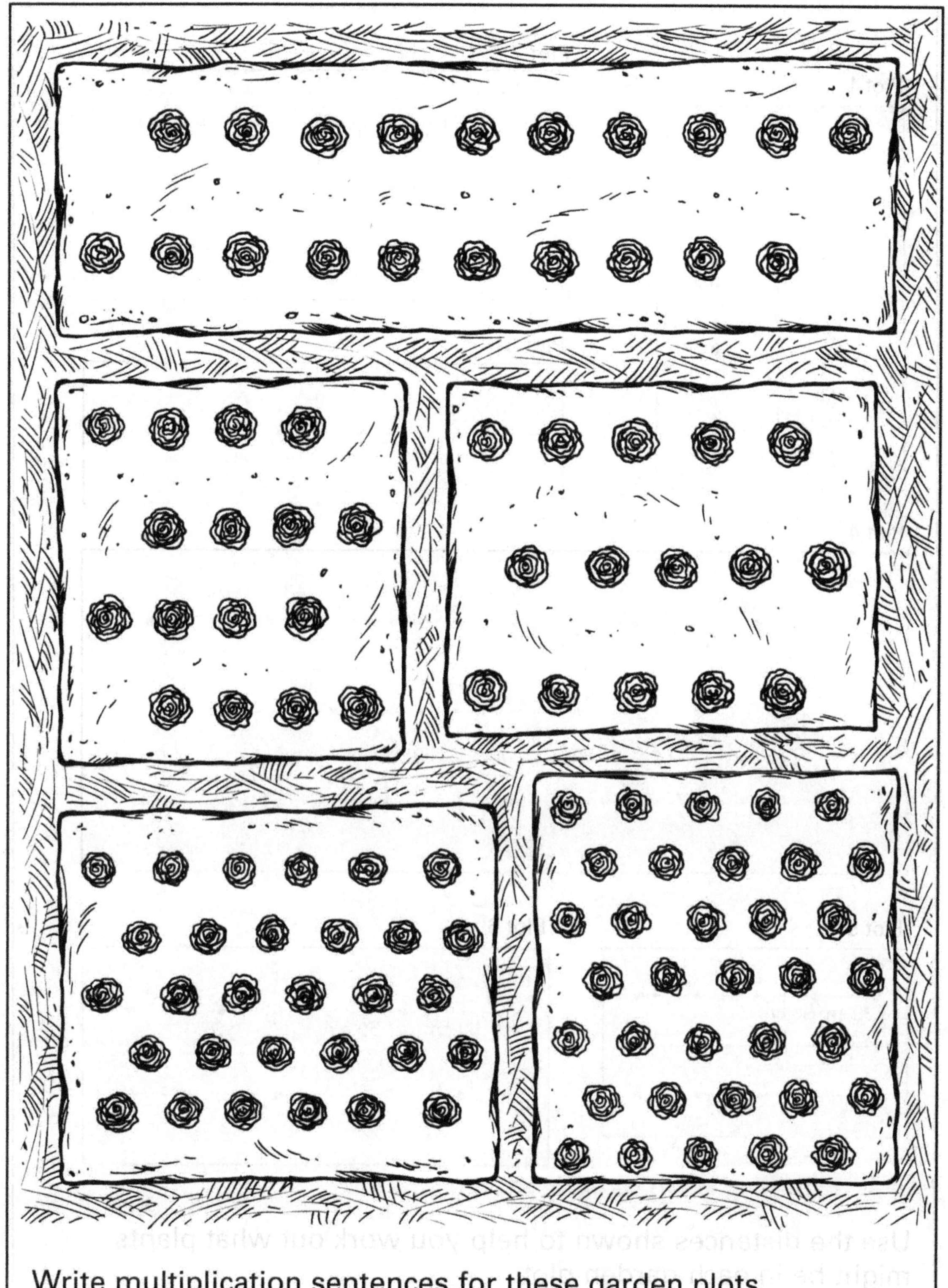

Write multiplication sentences for these garden plots.

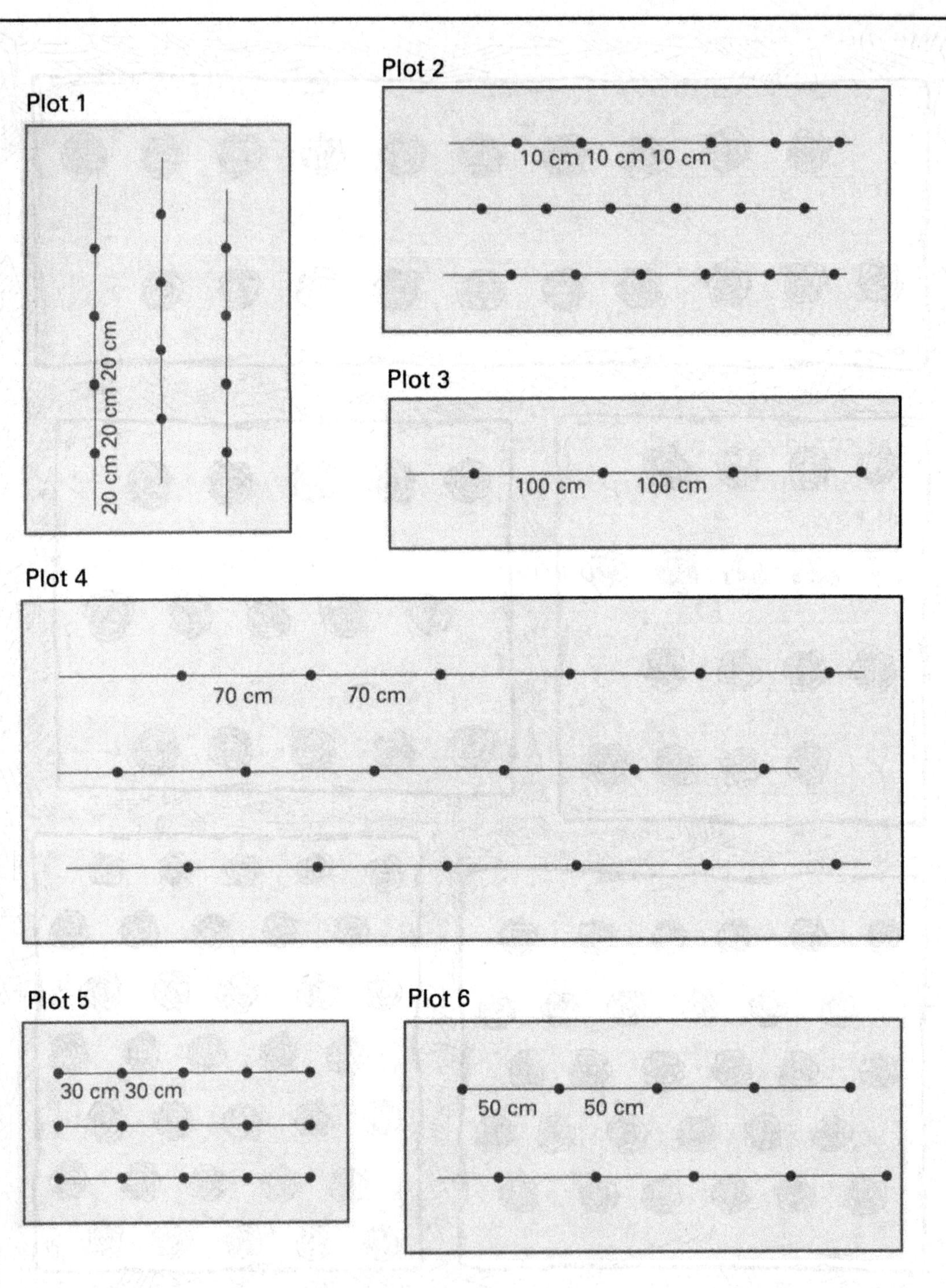

Use the distances shown to help you work out what plants might be in each garden plot.

0
20
40
60
80

1 cm on this number line equals 20 cm in the bean plot. How many beans could we plant in this row? (No plant is placed at the beginning or end of the row.)

What scale is used on each of the following number lines? Use the scale and a ruler to work out how many plants will be in each row.

0
30
60
90
120

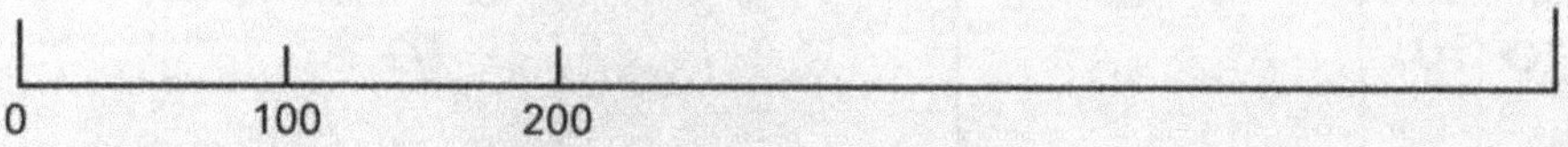
0
100
200

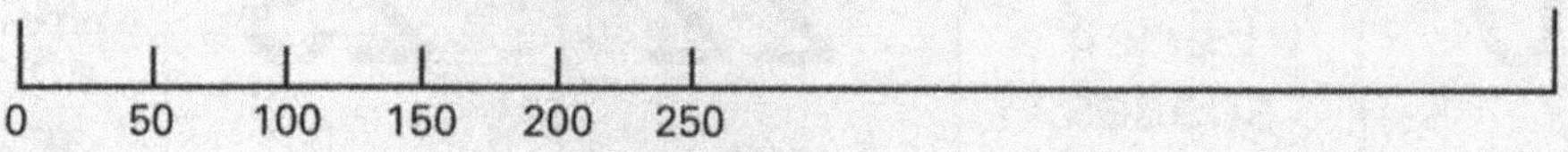
0
50
100
150
200
250

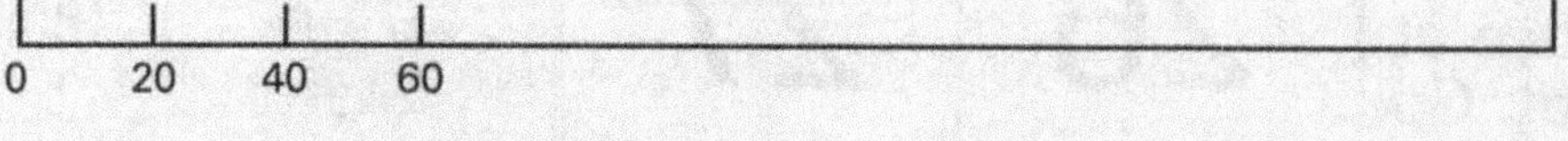
0
20
40
60

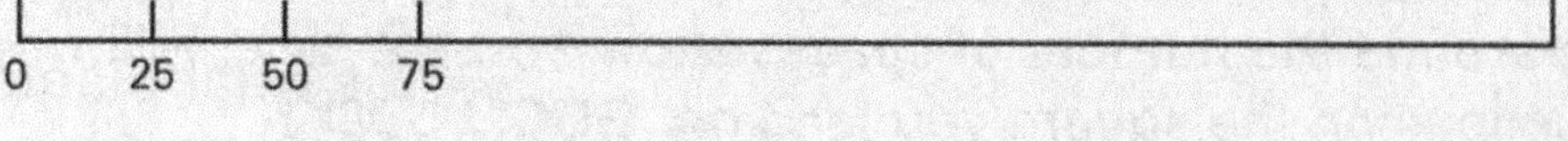
0
25
50
75

START	1	2	Pigs destroy banana crop. Return to start.	4
5	Price of coffee doubles. Go ahead 3 spaces.	7	8	Floods ruin crops. Return to start.
10	11	Rainy season comes early. Go to 16.	13	14
Rascals steal coffee beans. Go back to 10.	16	17	Family help with the harvest. Go to 23.	19
20	Brideprice feast. Go back 4 spaces.	22	23	Village buys truck. Go ahead 3 spaces.
Get high price for produce at market. Go to 27.	26	27	Local volcano erupts. Start again.	FINISH

RULES: Place your counter on the START. Take turns to throw the dice. Move around the number of spaces shown on the dice. Follow any instructions on the square you land on. GOOD LUCK!

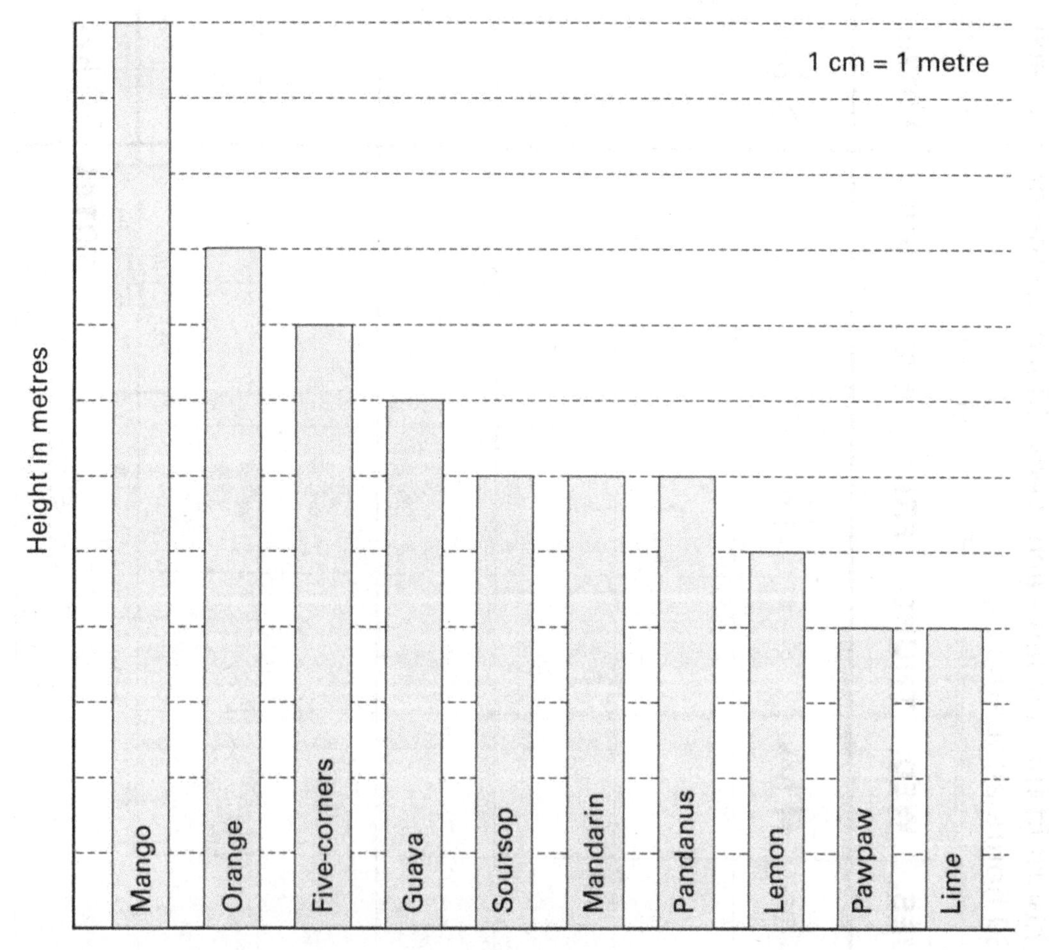

Types of trees

1. Name three trees that grow taller than 6 metres.
2. How tall does the orange tree grow?
3. Which trees grow 6 metres high?
4. How tall does your favourite fruit tree grow?
5. Which trees grow less than 6 metres tall?
6. Find something which is the same height as the orange tree.

This family spends a total of 30 hours in the garden each week. Make up the hours each person works to give a total of 30 hours altogether.

	MON.	TUES.	WED.	THURS.	FRI.	SAT.	SUN.	TOTAL
MUM	2 hrs	1 hr	4 hrs		1 hr			8 hrs
DAD								
GRANDMA								
KILA								
SARUA								
BABY								
							TOTAL	30 hrs

A
Use the length shown for each pole to estimate the height and width of the tree next to it.
2m
B
1m
D
C
2m
3m

How many leaves do you think this tree has?

pawpaw pineapple five corner banana

How much does each piece of fruit weigh? Choose the correct answer.

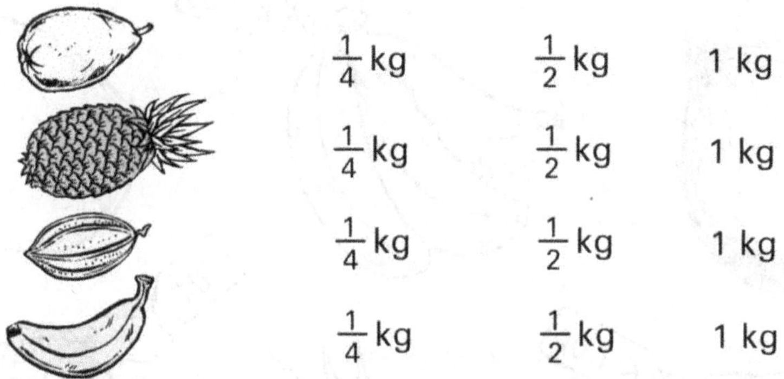

pawpaw	$\frac{1}{4}$ kg	$\frac{1}{2}$ kg	1 kg
pineapple	$\frac{1}{4}$ kg	$\frac{1}{2}$ kg	1 kg
five corner	$\frac{1}{4}$ kg	$\frac{1}{2}$ kg	1 kg
banana	$\frac{1}{4}$ kg	$\frac{1}{2}$ kg	1 kg

How much does the fruit in each basket weigh?

Draw 2 baskets and fill each with fruit weighing a total of 2 kg.

How many of each fruit or vegetable can you buy for K2.00?

60t

K 1.00

30t

90t

K 1.00

K 2.00

70t

K 1.00

80t

K 1.00

Draw clock-faces to show what time each of these events takes place.

In your exercise book, for each Frame write the names of all the items in each circle. Then, add those items from outside each circle that belong in the same group. Then, write the rule for belonging to the group.

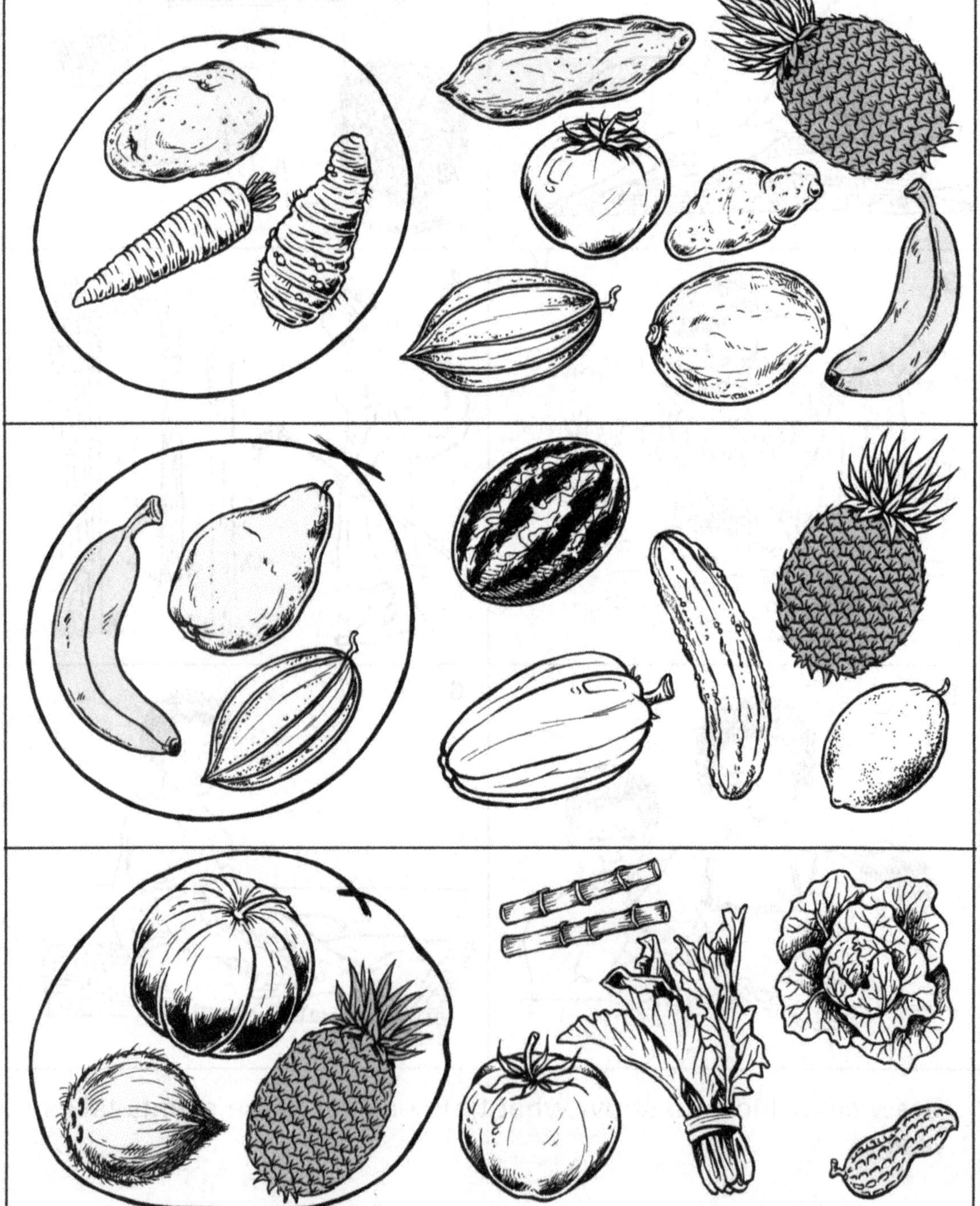

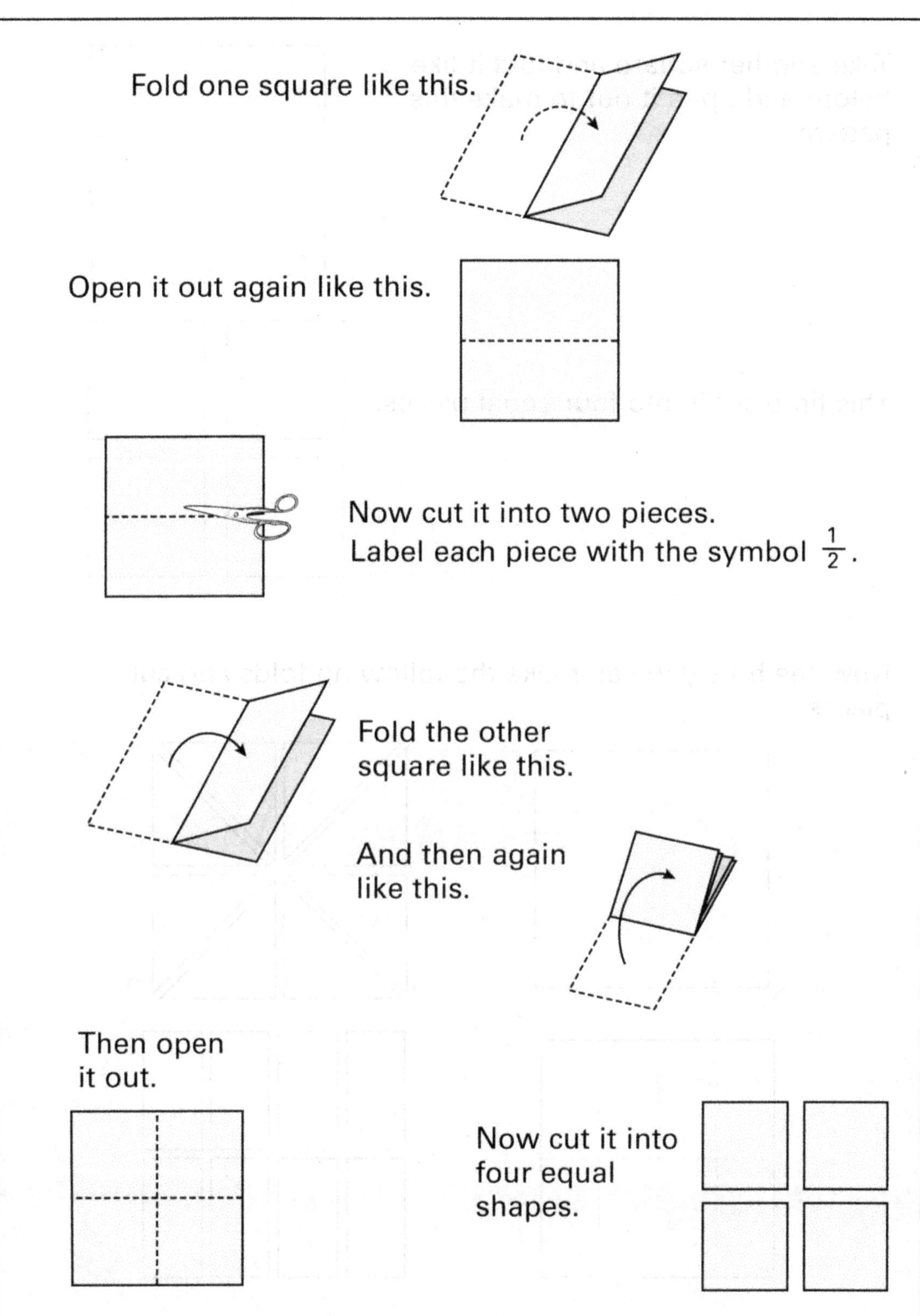
Fold one square like this.
Open it out again like this.
Now cut it into two pieces.
Label each piece with the symbol $\frac{1}{2}$.
Fold the other square like this.
And then again like this.
Then open it out.
Now cut it into four equal shapes.

Take another square and fold it like before and open it out to make this pattern.

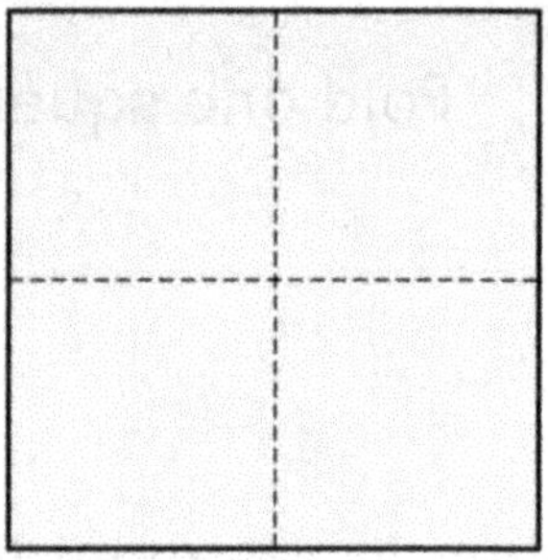

This time cut it into four equal pieces.

Now see how you can make the following folds and cut pieces.

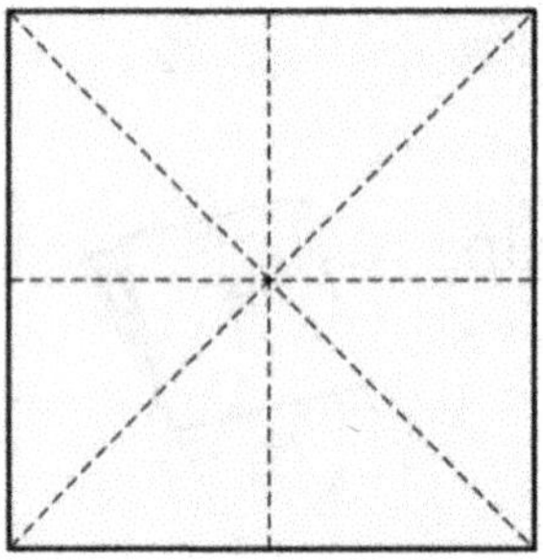

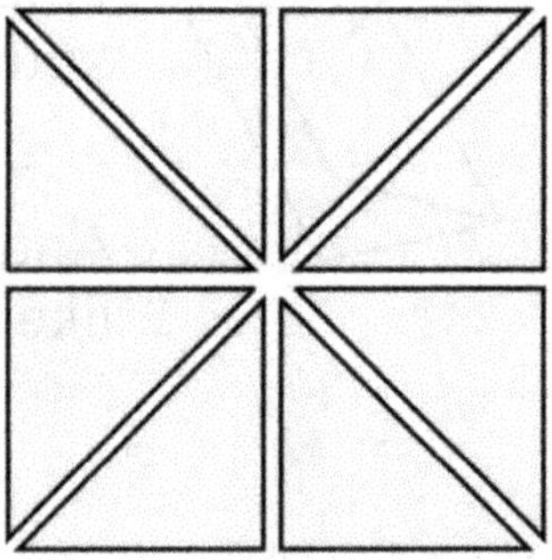

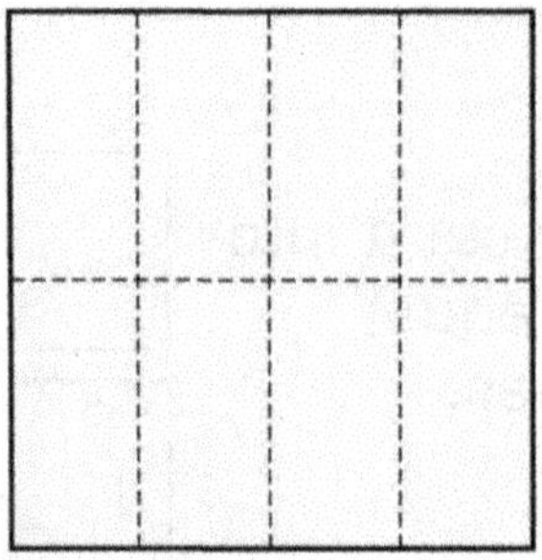